SECRET CHURCH

WHO AM I?

STUDY GUIDE

ISBN 979-8-9855655-0-8

Published by Radical, Inc.

TABLE OF CONTENTS

WHO AM I?

WHO AM I?

Then God said, "Let us make man in our image, after our likeness. And let them have dominion over the fish of the sea and over the birds of the heavens and over the livestock and over all the earth and over every creeping thing that creeps on the earth." So God created man in his own image, in the image of God he created him; male and female he created them. And God blessed them. And God said to them, "Be fruitful and multiply and fill the earth and subdue it, and have dominion over the fish of the sea and over the birds of the heavens and over every living thing that moves on the earth." (Genesis 1:26–28)

"These words, 'made in the image of God,' form the fundamental definition of who we are. The story of humanity and all it was meant to be and do begins with these words. Captured in these words are human identity, human meaning and purpose, the definition of how humans are to function, and a finger pointing to human destiny. The narrative of humanity is captured by these words. Here is the all-encompassing and inescapable human identity. It is stamped by the Creator on everyone. By his good and wise will, this is who God has chosen us to be. All other identity markers are subservient to this one. 'Like God.' There is no more basic thing that you could say about every human being that has ever lived." – Paul David Tripp[1]

This question is intimately _____.

> *Now when Jesus came into the district of Caesarea Philippi, he asked his disciples, "Who do people say that the Son of Man is?" And they said, "Some say John the Baptist, others say Elijah, and others Jeremiah or one of the prophets." He said to them, "But who do you say that I am?" Simon Peter replied, "You are the Christ, the Son of the living God." And Jesus answered him, "Blessed are you, Simon Bar-Jonah! For flesh and blood has not revealed this to you, but my Father who is in heaven. And I tell you, you are Peter, and on this rock I will build my church, and the gates of hell shall not prevail against it." (Matthew 16:13–18)*

"The concept of the image of God reveals the pattern for the people of God that clarifies both who the people of God are and what the mission is of the people of God." – Juan Sanchez[2]

This question is extremely _____.

- It defines our understanding of gender and sexuality.

  "The language around gender and sexuality continues to evolve rapidly, even as this resolution was being written. Words and their definitions change or become refined as our understanding of complex constructs related to sexuality and gender evolves. We recognize that learning which words or phrases are most accurate, respectful and useful is an important goal in adopting this resolution. Given how rapidly terminology changes, we recognize that even this list of terms and definitions might undergo significant change in the future. Therefore, it is important to explicitly and consciously articulate our current understanding of the following terms that appear in this resolution and in its supporting documents: Asexual, Bullying, Cisgender, DSD, Gender, Gender Expression, Gender Identity, Gender Diversity, Gender Dysphoria, Gender Identity, Gender Non-Conforming, Gender Role, Genderqueer, Intersex, Pansexual, Pushout, Queer, Questioning, Sex, Sex Assignment, Sexual Orientation, Transgender." – American Psychological Association, Division of School Psychology, and Society for the Psychological Study of LGBT Issues[3]

- It drives our perspective on race and justice.

  "If the Church of today does not recapture the sacrificial spirit of the early Church, it will lose its authentic ring, forfeit the loyalty of millions, and be dismissed as an irrelevant social club with no meaning for the twentieth century." – Martin Luther King, Jr.[4]

- It shapes our approach to technology.

○ The Metaverse

> "Humans of the Metaverse is a collection of 6,500 unique Meta Humans NFTs, stored as ERC-721 tokens on the Ethereum blockchain and hosted on IPFS. Each resident of the Metaverse will represent a unique composition from over 200 traits collected from the most notable and influential personalities aggregated from all temporal spaces. We are creating the Metacity—a fully integrated Web3 ecosystem where HOTM token holders will be able to spend $HOTM (our proprietary ERC-20 token) in an increasing number of ways, providing long-term value and utility to holders as the city grows." – Humans of the Metaverse[5]

> "The metaverse has been peddled as a futuristic place where we all—sitting in our living rooms with goggles strapped to our noggins—can interact, buy things, date, and more in a virtual world. But what if, in addition to being a place, the metaverse also represents something else: a point in time when we live more in the digital world than we do in the physical one?" – Katie Canales, *Business Insider*[6]

• Artificial Intelligence

> "The development of full artificial intelligence could spell the end of the human race. . . . It would take off on its own, and re-design itself at an ever increasing rate. . . . Humans, who are limited by slow biological evolution, couldn't compete, and would be superseded." – Stephen Hawking[7]

> "The human species can, if it wishes, transcend itself—not just sporadically, an individual here in one way, an individual there in another way, but in its entirety, as humanity." – Julian Huxley[8]

• It influences our use of science.

○ Genomics

> "We did it! . . . We genetically engineered an embryo! Our humanity has just been changed forever! . . . I view it as one of

the most groundbreaking things that's been done in science. In all of human history, we didn't get to decide what genes we have, right? Now we do. . . . For days I was so excited I couldn't sleep, because it affirmed to me why I do what I do, which is to try to make sure that people can push humanity forward."
– Josiah Zayner[9]

"After more than three billion years of evolution of life on this planet, one species (us) had developed the talent and temerity to grab control of its own genetic future. There [is] a sense that we [have] crossed the threshold into a whole new age, perhaps a brave new world, like when Adam and Eve bit into the apple. . . . "
– Walter Isaacson[10]

"Should we edit our species to make us less susceptible to deadly viruses? What a wonderful boon that would be! Right? Should we use gene editing to eliminate dreaded disorders, such as Huntington's, sickle-cell anemia, and cystic fibrosis? That sounds good, too. And what about deafness or blindness? Or being short? Or depressed? Hmmm . . . How should we think about that? A few decades from now, if it becomes possible and safe, should we allow parents to enhance the IQ and muscles of their kids? Should we let them decide eye color? Skin color? Height? Whoa! Let's pause for a moment before we slide all of the way down this slippery slope. What might that do to the diversity of our societies? If we are no longer subject to a random natural lottery when it comes to our endowments, will it weaken our feelings of empathy and acceptance? If these offerings at the genetic supermarket aren't free (and they won't be), will that greatly increase inequality—and indeed encode it permanently in the human race? Given these issues, should such decisions be left solely to individuals, or should society as a whole have some say? Perhaps we should develop some rules.

By 'we' I mean we. All of us, including you and me. Figuring out if and when to edit our genes will be one of the most consequential questions of the twenty-first century." – Walter Isaacson[11]

○ Eugenics

> " . . . the demand that defective people be prevented from propagating equally defective offspring is a demand of the clearest reason and if systematically executed represents the most humane act of mankind." – Adolf Hitler[12]

> "The emergency problem of segregation and sterilization must be faced immediately. Every feeble-minded girl or woman of the hereditary type, especially of the moron class, should be segregated during the reproductive period. Otherwise, she is almost certain to bear imbecile children, who in turn are just as certain to breed other defectives. . . . Moreover, when we realize that each feeble-minded person is a potential source of an endless progeny of defect, we prefer the policy of immediate sterilization, of making sure that parenthood is absolutely prohibited to the feeble-minded." – Margaret Sanger[13]

This question is ultimately consequential.

• For life on this _earth_ .

• For life in _eternity_ .

> And just as it is appointed for man to die once, and after that comes judgment, so Christ, having been offered once to bear the sins of many, will appear a second time, not to deal with sin but to save those who are eagerly waiting for him. (Hebrews 9:27–28)

Our Plan

• Epic Questions
    ○ Who am I? (Who are we?)
    ○ What is wrong in the world?
    ○ How can it be made right? How can I (how can we) experience the good life?

- Contemporary Applications
  - Humanity and Sexuality
  - Humanity and Race
  - Humanity and Abortion
  - Humanity, Infertility, and Artificial Reproductive Technology
  - Humanity, Genomics, and Eugenics
  - Humanity and Artificial Intelligence
  - Humanity, Digital and Social Media, and the Metaverse
- Ultimate Conclusions
  - Who is God?
- Along the Way
  - Biblical Meditation
  - Theological Foundations
  - Intentional Reflection

only humans are created
in His image

Genesis 1:26–31

26 Then God said, "Let us make man in our image, after our likeness. And let them have dominion over the fish of the sea and over the birds of the heavens and over the livestock and over all the earth and over every creeping thing that creeps on the earth." 27 So God created man in his own image, in the image of God he created him; male and female he created them. 28 And God blessed them. And God said to them, "Be fruitful and multiply and fill the earth and subdue it, and have dominion over the fish of the sea and over the birds of the heavens and over every living thing that moves on the earth." 29 And God said, "Behold, I have given you every plant yielding seed that is on the face of all the earth, and every tree with seed in its fruit. You shall have them for food. 30 And to every beast of the earth and to every bird of the heavens and to everything that creeps on the earth, everything that has the breath of life, I have given every green plant for food." And it was so. 31 And God saw everything that he had made, and behold, it was very good. And there was evening and there was morning, the sixth day.

Psalm 8:1-9 *[handwritten: Yaweh → Adam "King"]*

[1] O LORD, our Lord, how majestic is your name in all the

earth! You have set your glory above the heavens. [2] Out

of the mouth of babies and infants, you have established

strength because of your foes, to still the enemy and the

avenger. [3] When I look at your heavens, the work of your

fingers, the moon and the stars, which you have set in

place, [4] what is man that you are mindful of him, and the

son of man that you care for him? [5] Yet you have made him

a little lower than the heavenly beings and crowned him

with glory and honor. [6] You have given him dominion over

the works of your hands; you have put all things under his

feet, [7] all sheep and oxen, and also the beasts of the field,

[8] the birds of the heavens, and the fish of the sea, whatever

passes along the paths of the seas. [9] O LORD, our Lord,

how majestic is your name in all the earth!

Revelation 22:1–5

[1] Then the angel showed me the river of the water of life, bright as crystal, flowing from the throne of God and of the Lamb [2] through the middle of the street of the city; also, on either side of the river, the tree of life with its twelve kinds of fruit, yielding its fruit each month. The leaves of the tree were for the healing of the nations. [3] No longer will there be anything accursed, but the throne of God and of the Lamb will be in it, and his servants will worship him. [4] They will see his face, and his name will be on their foreheads. [5] And night will be no more. They will need no light of lamp or sun, for the Lord God will be their light, and they will reign forever and ever.

EPIC
QUESTIONS

WHO AM I? (WHO ARE WE?)[14]

> **I am a man or a woman personally made by God in the image of God to enjoy and exalt the glory of God.**

I am . . . personally made by God . . .

For you formed my inward parts; you knitted me together in my mother's womb. I praise you, for I am fearfully and wonderfully made. Wonderful are your works; my soul knows it very well. My frame was not hidden from you, when I was being made in secret, intricately woven in the depths of the earth. Your eyes saw my unformed substance; in your book were written, every one of them, the days that were formed for me, when as yet there was none of them. (Psalm 139:13–16)

God is Creator; we are creatures.

In the beginning, God created the heavens and the earth. (Genesis 1:1)

So God created man in his own image, in the image of God he created him; male and female he created them. (Genesis 1:27)

God is independent; we are dependent.

God said to Moses, "I AM WHO I AM." And he said, "Say this to the people of Israel: 'I AM has sent me to you.'" God also said to Moses, "Say this to the people of Israel: 'The LORD, the God of your fathers, the God of Abraham, the God of Isaac, and the God of Jacob, has sent me to you.' This is my name forever, and thus I am to be remembered throughout all generations." (Exodus 3:14–15)

For by him all things were created, in heaven and on earth, visible and invisible, whether thrones or dominions or rulers or authorities— all things were created through him and for him. And he is before all things, and in him all things hold together. (Colossians 1:16–17)

God is sovereign; we are subordinate.

You are the LORD, you alone. You have made heaven, the heaven of heavens, with all their host, the earth and all that is on it, the seas and all that is in them; and you preserve all of them; and the host of heaven worships you. (Nehemiah 9:6)

The earth is the LORD's and the fullness thereof, the world and those who dwell therein . . . (Psalm 24:1)

God is authoritative; we are ___*accountable*___

The LORD God took the man and put him in the garden of Eden to work it and keep it. And the LORD God commanded the man, saying, "You may surely eat of every tree of the garden, but of the tree of the knowledge of good and evil you shall not eat, for in the day that you eat of it you shall surely die." (Genesis 2:15–17)

Now we know that whatever the law says it speaks to those who are under the law, so that every mouth may be stopped, and the whole world may be held accountable to God. For by works of the law no human being will be justified in his sight, since through the law comes knowledge of sin. (Romans 3:19–20)

God is in charge; we make choices.

But Joseph said to them, "Do not fear, for am I in the place of God? As for you, you meant evil against me, but God meant it for good, to bring it about that many people should be kept alive, as they are today." (Genesis 50:19–20)

. . . this Jesus, delivered up according to the definite plan and foreknowledge of God, you crucified and killed by the hands of lawless men. (Acts 2:23)

When they were released, they went to their friends and reported what the chief priests and the elders had said to them. And when they heard it, they lifted their voices together to God and said, "Sovereign Lord, who made the heaven and the earth and the sea and everything in them, who through the mouth of our father David, your servant, said by the Holy Spirit, 'Why did the Gentiles rage, and the peoples plot in vain? The kings of the earth set themselves, and the rulers were gathered together, against the Lord and against his Anointed'—for truly in this city there were gathered together against your holy servant Jesus, whom you anointed, both Herod and Pontius Pilate, along with the Gentiles and the peoples of Israel, to do whatever your hand and your plan had predestined to take place. And now, Lord, look upon their threats and grant to your servants to continue to speak your word with all boldness, while you stretch out your hand to heal, and signs and wonders are performed through the name of your holy servant Jesus." And when they had prayed, the place in which they were gathered together was shaken, and they were all filled with the Holy Spirit and continued to speak the word of God with boldness. (Acts 4:23–31)

God is love; we are beloved.

So we have come to know and to believe the love that God has for us. God is love, and whoever abides in love abides in God, and God abides in him. (1 John 4:16)

For God so loved the world, that he gave his only Son, that whoever believes in him should not perish but have eternal life. (John 3:16)

. . . to enjoy and exalt the glory of God.

Life is found in _____ God in all of his glory.

> The thief comes only to steal and kill and destroy. I came that they may have life and have it abundantly. (John 10:10)

> And this is eternal life, that they know you, the only true God, and Jesus Christ whom you have sent. (John 17:3)

- We delight in God.

> You make known to me the path of life; in your presence there is fullness of joy; at your right hand are pleasures forevermore. (Psalm 16:11)

> One thing have I asked of the LORD, that will I seek after: that I may dwell in the house of the LORD all the days of my life, to gaze upon the beauty of the LORD and to inquire in his temple. (Psalm 27:4)

- God delights in us.

> For as a young man marries a young woman, so shall your sons marry you, and as the bridegroom rejoices over the bride, so shall your God rejoice over you. (Isaiah 62:5)

> The LORD your God is in your midst, a mighty one who will save; he will rejoice over you with gladness; he will quiet you by his love; he will exult over you with loud singing. I will gather those of you who mourn for the festival, so that you will no longer suffer reproach. (Zephaniah 3:17–18)

Life is found in _____ God in all of his glory.

> But now thus says the LORD, he who created you, O Jacob, he who formed you, O Israel: "Fear not, for I have redeemed you; I have called you by name, you are mine. When you pass through the waters,

I will be with you; and through the rivers, they shall not overwhelm you; when you walk through fire you shall not be burned, and the flame shall not consume you. For I am the LORD your God, the Holy One of Israel, your Savior. I give Egypt as your ransom, Cush and Seba in exchange for you. Because you are precious in my eyes, and honored, and I love you, I give men in return for you, peoples in exchange for your life. Fear not, for I am with you; I will bring your offspring from the east, and from the west I will gather you. I will say to the north, Give up, and to the south, Do not withhold; bring my sons from afar and my daughters from the end of the earth, everyone who is called by my name, whom I created for my glory, whom I formed and made." (Isaiah 43:1–7)

For from him and through him and to him are all things. To him be glory forever. Amen. (Romans 11:36)

Worthy are you, our Lord and God, to receive glory and honor and power, for you created all things, and by your will they existed and were created. (Revelation 4:11)

- In everything we do.

  So, whether you eat or drink, or whatever you do, do all to the glory of God. (1 Corinthians 10:31)

- To the ends of the earth.

  But you will receive power when the Holy Spirit has come upon you, and you will be my witnesses in Jerusalem and in all Judea and Samaria, and to the end of the earth. (Acts 1:8)

  And they sang a new song, saying, "Worthy are you to take the scroll and to open its seals, for you were slain, and by your blood you ransomed people for God from every tribe and language and people and nation, and you have made them a kingdom and priests to our God, and they shall reign on the earth." Then I looked, and I heard around the throne and the living creatures and the elders the voice of many angels, numbering myriads of myriads and thousands of thousands, saying with a loud voice,

"Worthy is the Lamb who was slain, to receive power and wealth and wisdom and might and honor and glory and blessing!" And I heard every creature in heaven and on earth and under the earth and in the sea, and all that is in them, saying, "To him who sits on the throne and to the Lamb be blessing and honor and glory and might forever and ever!" And the four living creatures said, "Amen!" and the elders fell down and worshiped. (Revelation 5:9–14)

. . . in the image of God . . .

Then God said, "Let us make man in our image, after our likeness. And let them have dominion over the fish of the sea and over the birds of the heavens and over the livestock and over all the earth and over every creeping thing that creeps on the earth." So God created man in his own image, in the image of God he created him; male and female he created them. And God blessed them. And God said to them, "Be fruitful and multiply and fill the earth and subdue it, and have dominion over the fish of the sea and over the birds of the heavens and over every living thing that moves on the earth." (Genesis 1:26–28)

Humanity resembles God.

When Adam had lived 130 years, he fathered a son in his own likeness, after his image, and named him Seth. (Genesis 5:3)

- We resemble God _Spiritually_

God is spirit, and those who worship him must worship in spirit and truth. (John 4:24)

  - We are spiritual beings with bodies.

    Thus says God, the LORD, who created the heavens and stretched them out, who spread out the earth and what comes

> from it, who gives breath to the people on it and spirit to those who walk in it . . . (Isaiah 42:5)

> Now while Paul was waiting for them at Athens, his spirit was provoked within him as he saw that the city was full of idols. (Acts 17:16)

> After saying these things, Jesus was troubled in his spirit, and testified, "Truly, truly, I say to you, one of you will betray me." (John 13:21)

> The Spirit himself bears witness with our spirit that we are children of God . . . (Romans 8:16)

○ We are influenced by spiritual beings without bodies.

> When the servant of the man of God rose early in the morning and went out, behold, an army with horses and chariots was all around the city. And the servant said, "Alas, my master! What shall we do?" He said, "Do not be afraid, for those who are with us are more than those who are with them." Then Elisha prayed and said, "O Lord, please open his eyes that he may see." So the Lord opened the eyes of the young man, and he saw, and behold, the mountain was full of horses and chariots of fire all around Elisha. And when the Syrians came down against him, Elisha prayed to the Lord and said, "Please strike this people with blindness." So he struck them with blindness in accordance with the prayer of Elisha. (2 Kings 6:15–18)

- Demons work to harm us.

> Finally, be strong in the Lord and in the strength of his might. Put on the whole armor of God, that you may be able to stand against the schemes of the devil. For we do not wrestle against flesh and blood, but against the rulers, against the authorities, against the cosmic powers over this present darkness, against the spiritual forces of evil in the heavenly places. (Ephesians 6:10–12)

- Angels work to help us.

  > *For he will command his angels concerning you to guard you in all your ways. On their hands they will bear you up, lest you strike your foot against a stone.* (Psalm 91:11–12)

  > *Then the devil left him, and behold, angels came and were ministering to him.* (Matthew 4:11)

○ Our spirits will never die.

  > *He has made everything beautiful in its time. Also, he has put eternity into man's heart, yet so that he cannot find out what God has done from the beginning to the end.* (Ecclesiastes 3:11)

  > *So we are always of good courage. We know that while we are at home in the body we are away from the Lord, for we walk by faith, not by sight. Yes, we are of good courage, and we would rather be away from the body and at home with the Lord. So whether we are at home or away, we make it our aim to please him. For we must all appear before the judgment seat of Christ, so that each one may receive what is due for what he had done in the body, whether good or evil.* (2 Corinthians 5:6–10)

- We resemble God _____.

  > *God is spirit, and those who worship him must worship in spirit and truth.* (John 4:24)

  ○ We reflect God's spiritual qualities in our physical bodies.
    - God sees, and our bodies enable us to see.

      > *For the eyes of the LORD run to and fro throughout the whole earth, to give strong support to those whose heart is blameless toward him.* (2 Chronicles 16:9a)

    - God hears, and our bodies enable us to hear.

> *I cried to him with my mouth, and high praise was on my tongue. If I had cherished iniquity in my heart, the Lord would not have listened. But truly God has listened; he has attended to the voice of my prayer. Blessed be God, because he has not rejected my prayer or removed his steadfast love from me!* (Psalm 66:17–20)

> *And this is the confidence that we have toward him, that if we ask anything according to his will he hears us. And if we know that he hears us in whatever we ask, we know that we have the requests that we have asked of him.* (1 John 5:14–15)

- God speaks, and our bodies enable us to speak.

> *And God said, "Let there be light," and there was light.* (Genesis 1:3)

> *And the LORD God commanded the man, saying, "You may surely eat of every tree of the garden, but of the tree of the knowledge of good and evil you shall not eat, for in the day that you eat of it you shall surely die."* (Genesis 2:16–17)

○ We imitate God's spiritual qualities in our physical bodies.

> *Therefore be imitators of God, as beloved children.* (Ephesians 5:1)

> *. . . since it is written, "You shall be holy, for I am holy."* (1 Peter 1:16)

○ Soul __and__ body.

> *. . . then the Lord God formed the man of dust from the ground and breathed into his nostrils the breath of life, and the man became a living creature.* (Genesis 2:7)

> *. . . and his interests are divided. And the unmarried or betrothed woman is anxious about the things of the Lord,*

how to be holy in body and spirit. But the married woman is anxious about worldly things, how to please her husband. (1 Corinthians 7:34)

Since we have these promises, beloved, let us cleanse ourselves from every defilement of body and spirit, bringing holiness to completion in the fear of God. (2 Corinthians 7:1)

- Is it soul/spirit or soul *and* spirit?

Now is my soul troubled. And what shall I say? "Father, save me from this hour"? But for this purpose I have come to this hour. (John 12:27)

And Mary said, "My soul magnifies the Lord, and my spirit rejoices in God my Savior . . ." (Luke 1:46–47)

. . . and to the assembly of the firstborn who are enrolled in heaven, and to God, the judge of all, and to the spirits of the righteous made perfect . . . (Hebrews 12:23)

When he opened the fifth seal, I saw under the altar the souls of those who had been slain for the word of God and for the witness they had borne. (Revelation 6:9)

When Jesus had received the sour wine, he said, "It is finished," and he bowed his head and gave up his spirit. (John 19:30)

And as they were stoning Stephen, he called out, "Lord Jesus, receive my spirit." (Acts 7:59)

And do not fear those who kill the body but cannot kill the soul. Rather fear him who can destroy both soul and body in hell. (Matthew 10:28)

. . . you are to deliver this man to Satan for the destruction of the flesh, so that his spirit may be saved in the day of the Lord. (1 Corinthians 5:5)

- Our souls/spirits work in coordination with our bodies.

> And you shall love the Lord your God with all your heart and with all your soul and with all your mind and with all your strength. (Mark 12:30)

> O God, you are my God; earnestly I seek you; my soul thirsts for you; my flesh faints for you, as in a dry and weary land where there is no water. (Psalm 63:1)

> My soul longs, yes, faints for the courts of the LORD; my heart and flesh sing for joy to the living God. (Psalm 84:2)

- Our souls/spirits can exist apart from our bodies.

> And he said to him, "Truly, I say to you, today you will be with me in paradise." (Luke 23:43)

> When he opened the fifth seal, I saw under the altar the souls of those who had been slain for the word of God and for the witness they had borne. They cried out with a loud voice, "O Sovereign Lord, holy and true, how long before you will judge and avenge our blood on those who dwell on the earth?" (Revelation 6:9–10)

- We resemble God _____.

> I am speaking the truth in Christ—I am not lying; my conscience bears me witness in the Holy Spirit . . . (Romans 9:1)

> Now concerning food offered to idols: we know that "all of us possess knowledge." This "knowledge" puffs up, but love builds up. If anyone imagines that he knows something, he does not yet know as he ought to know. But if anyone loves God, he is known by God. (1 Corinthians 8:1–3)

> Thus, sinning against your brothers and wounding their conscience when it is weak, you sin against Christ. (1 Corinthians 8:12)

- We are able to reason and remember.

> *Come now, let us reason together, says the Lord: though your sins are like scarlet, they shall be as white as snow; though they are red like crimson, they shall become like wool.* (Isaiah 1:18)

> *Remember the word that I said to you: "A servant is not greater than his master." If they persecuted me, they will also persecute you. If they kept my word, they will also keep yours.* (John 15:20)

- We are able to communicate in complex, abstract language.

> *And the rib that the LORD God had taken from the man he made into a woman and brought her to the man. Then the man said, "This at last is bone of my bones and flesh of my flesh; she shall be called Woman, because she was taken out of Man." Therefore a man shall leave his father and his mother and hold fast to his wife, and they shall become one flesh. And the man and his wife were both naked and were not ashamed. Now the serpent was more crafty than any other beast of the field that the LORD God had made. He said to the woman, "Did God actually say, 'You shall not eat of any tree in the garden'?" And the woman said to the serpent, "We may eat of the fruit of the trees in the garden, but God said, 'You shall not eat of the fruit of the tree that is in the midst of the garden, neither shall you touch it, lest you die.'" But the serpent said to the woman, "You will not surely die. For God knows that when you eat of it your eyes will be opened, and you will be like God, knowing good and evil." So when the woman saw that the tree was good for food, and that it was a delight to the eyes, and that the tree was to be desired to make one wise, she took of its fruit and ate, and she also gave some to her husband who was with her, and he ate.* (Genesis 2:22–3:6)

- We have an awareness of the future.

> *He has made everything beautiful in its time. Also, he has put eternity into man's heart, yet so that he cannot find out what God has done from the beginning to the end.* (Ecclesiastes 3:11)

○ We have the capacity to create.

> At the end of forty days Noah opened the window of the ark that
> he had made . . . (Genesis 8:6)

> Then they said, "Come, let us build ourselves a city and a
> tower with its top in the heavens, and let us make a name for
> ourselves, lest we be dispersed over the face of the whole earth."
> (Genesis 11:4)

- ▪ God creates from nothing.

> By faith we understand that the universe was created by
> the word of God, so that what is seen was not made out of
> things that are visible. (Hebrews 11:3)

> . . . as it is written, "I have made you the father of many
> nations"—in the presence of the God in whom he believed,
> who gives life to the dead and calls into existence the things
> that do not exist. (Romans 4:17)

- ▪ We create from something.

> The LORD said to Moses, "See, I have called by name
> Bezalel the son of Uri, son of Hur, of the tribe of Judah,
> and I have filled him with the Spirit of God, with ability and
> intelligence, with knowledge and all craftsmanship, to devise
> artistic designs, to work in gold, silver, and bronze, in cutting
> stones for setting, and in carving wood, to work in every
> craft. And behold, I have appointed with him Oholiab, the
> son of Ahisamach, of the tribe of Dan. And I have given to
> all able men ability, that they may make all that I have
> commanded you . . ." (Exodus 31:1–6)

- We resemble God _____.

> . . . the LORD appeared to him from far away. I have loved
> you with an everlasting love; therefore I have continued my
> faithfulness to you. (Jeremiah 31:3)

As a father shows compassion to his children, so the LORD shows compassion to those who fear him. (Psalm 103:13)

There are six things that the LORD hates, seven that are an abomination to him . . . (Proverbs 6:16)

I will rejoice in doing them good, and I will plant them in this land in faithfulness, with all my heart and all my soul. (Jeremiah 32:41)

How often they rebelled against him in the wilderness and grieved him in the desert! (Psalm 78:40)

○ Our emotions are deeply personal.

When he arrived, Eli was sitting on his seat by the road watching, for his heart trembled for the ark of God. And when the man came into the city and told the news, all the city cried out. (1 Samuel 4:13)

In the morning, when the wine had gone out of Nabal, his wife told him these things, and his heart died within him, and he became as a stone. (1 Samuel 25:37)

I am poured out like water, and all my bones are out of joint; my heart is like wax; it is melted within my breast . . . (Psalm 22:14)

My heart staggers; horror has appalled me; the twilight I longed for has been turned for me into trembling. (Isaiah 21:4)

○ Our emotions are intricately complex.

He said to his brothers, "My money has been put back; here it is in the mouth of my sack!" At this their hearts failed them, and they turned trembling to one another, saying, "What is this that God has done to us?" (Genesis 42:28)

And as soon as we heard it, our hearts melted, and there was no spirit left in any man because of you, for the LORD your God, he is God in the heavens above and on the earth beneath. (Joshua 2:11)

Anxiety in a man's heart weighs him down, but a good word makes him glad. (Proverbs 12:25)

A glad heart makes a cheerful face, but by sorrow of heart the spirit is crushed. (Proverbs 15:13)

- We resemble God _____.

Far be it from you to do such a thing, to put the righteous to death with the wicked, so that the righteous fare as the wicked! Far be that from you! Shall not the Judge of all the earth do what is just? (Genesis 18:25)

  - We are aware of right and wrong.

For all who have sinned without the law will also perish without the law, and all who have sinned under the law will be judged by the law. For it is not the hearers of the law who are righteous before God, but the doers of the law who will be justified. For when Gentiles, who do not have the law, by nature do what the law requires, they are a law to themselves, even though they do not have the law. They show that the work of the law is written on their hearts, while their conscience also bears witness, and their conflicting thoughts accuse or even excuse them on that day when, according to my gospel, God judges the secrets of men by Christ Jesus. (Romans 2:12–16)

  - We are accountable to God.

. . . but of the tree of the knowledge of good and evil you shall not eat, for in the day that you eat of it you shall surely die. (Genesis 2:17)

> *And I saw the dead, great and small, standing before the throne, and books were opened. Then another book was opened, which is the book of life. And the dead were judged by what was written in the books, according to what they had done.* (Revelation 20:12)

- We resemble God _____.
  - We have the ability to love God and others.

    > *And he said to him, "You shall love the Lord your God with all your heart and with all your soul and with all your mind. This is the great and first commandment. And a second is like it: You shall love your neighbor as yourself. On these two commandments depend all the Law and the Prophets."* (Matthew 22:37–40)

  - We have authority to rule under God with others.

    > *Yet you have made him a little lower than the heavenly beings and crowned him with glory and honor. You have given him dominion over the works of your hands; you have put all things under his feet, all sheep and oxen, and also the beasts of the field, the birds of the heavens, and the fish of the sea, whatever passes along the paths of the seas.* (Psalm 8:5–8)

- We resemble God incompletely.
  - God possesses some attributes that he does not share (or hardly shares) with us at all.
    - Independence.
      - God is both self-existent and self-sufficient.
      - The self-existence of God . . .
        - God was never created and never came into being.

          > *God said to Moses, "I AM WHO I AM." And he said, "Say this to the people of Israel: 'I AM has sent me to you.'"* (Exodus 3:14)

      - The self-sufficiency of God . . .
        - God has no needs.

> *The God who made the world and everything in it, being Lord of heaven and earth, does not live in temples made by man, nor is he served by human hands, as though he needed anything, since he himself gives to all mankind life and breath and everything.* (Acts 17:24–25)

- Eternity.
  - God is both infinite and eternal.
  - God as infinite . . .
    - God is unlimited and unlimitable, measureless and boundless.

      > *Can you find out the deep things of God? Can you find out the limit of the Almighty? It is higher than heaven—what can you do? Deeper than Sheol—what can you know?* (Job 11:7–8)

  - God as eternal . . .
    - God has no beginning or end; He transcends time, as Lord over time.

      > *LORD, you have been our dwelling place in all generations. Before the mountains were brought forth, or ever you had formed the earth and the world, from everlasting to everlasting you are God.* (Psalm 90:1–2)

- Omnipresence.
  - All of God is always present.

    > *Where shall I go from your Spirit? Or where shall I flee from your presence? If I ascend to heaven, you are there! If I make my bed in Sheol, you are there! If I take the wings of the morning and dwell in the uttermost parts of the sea, even there your hand shall lead me, and your right hand shall hold me.* (Psalm 139:7–10)

- Immutability.
  - The perfections, purposes, and promises of God are unchanging as he carries out his unfolding plan.

    > For I the LORD do not change; therefore you, O children of Jacob, are not consumed. (Malachi 3:6)

    > I am God, and there is none like me, declaring the end from the beginning and from ancient times things not yet done, saying, "My counsel shall stand, and I will accomplish all my purpose" . . . (Isaiah 46:9–10)

    > The grass withers, the flower fades, but the word of our God will stand forever. (Isaiah 40:8)

- God possesses others attributes that he shares with us in _____.
  - Spirituality.
    - God is both spiritual and personal.
    - God as spirit . . .
      - God is not physical, visible, or limited by space, size, or location.

        > God is spirit, and those who worship him must worship in spirit and truth. (John 4:24)

    - God as personal . . .
      - God is not a force to be reckoned with, or an object to be manipulated, but a personal Creator and Redeemer to be loved..

        > And he said to him, "You shall love the Lord your God with all your heart and with all your soul and with all your mind. This is the great and first commandment." (Matthew 22:37–38)

  - Omnipotence.
    - God has infinite power to do all things in his holy will.

> *Ah, Lord GOD! It is you who have made the heavens and the earth by your great power and by your outstretched arm! Nothing is too hard for you. (Jeremiah 32:17)*

> *Our God is in the heavens; he does all that he pleases. (Psalm 115:3)*

- Omniscience.
  - God has all knowledge and all wisdom at all times.

    > *Do you know the balancing of the clouds, the wondrous works of him who is perfect in knowledge . . . (Job 37:16)*

    > *To the only wise God be glory forevermore through Jesus Christ! Amen. (Romans 16:27)*

- Holiness.

  > *And one called to another and said: "Holy, holy, holy is the LORD of hosts; the whole earth is full of his glory!" (Isaiah 6:3)*

  - God is perfectly unique, completely separate, and absolutely pure (untouched by sin and intolerant of sin).

    > *There is none holy like the Lord: for there is none besides you; there is no rock like our God. (1 Samuel 2:2)*

    > *But as he who called you is holy, you also be holy in all your conduct, since it is written, "You shall be holy, for I am holy." (1 Peter 1:15–16)*

- Integrity.
  - God's genuineness: God is true.

    > *But the Lord is the true God; he is the living God and the everlasting King. (Jeremiah 10:10)*

  - God's veracity: God always tells the truth.

> *Every word of God proves true; he is a shield to those who take refuge in him. (Proverbs 30:5)*

- God's faithfulness: God always proves true.

  > *God is not man, that he should lie, or a son of man, that he should change his mind. Has he said, and will he not do it? Or has he spoken, and will he not fulfill it? (Numbers 23:19)*

- Love.

  > *So we have come to know and to believe the love that God has for us. God is love, and whoever abides in love abides in God, and God abides in him. (1 John 4:16)*

  - God eternally gives of himself and shares his gifts with others.

    > *Father, I desire that they also, whom you have given me, may be with me where I am, to see my glory that you have given me because you loved me before the foundation of the world. (John 17:24)*

- Mercy and Grace.
  - The mercy and grace of God are the love of God freely and sovereignly distributed by God amidst our sin and suffering.

    > *But God, being rich in mercy, because of the great love with which he loved us, even when we were dead in our trespasses, made us alive together with Christ—by grace you have been saved. (Ephesians 2:4–5)*

- Justice.
  - God administers his kingdom in accordance with his law.

    > *Give attention to me, my people, and give ear to me, my nation; for a law will go out from me, and I will set my*

> *justice for a light to the peoples. My righteousness draws near, my salvation has gone out, and my arms will judge the peoples; the coastlands hope for me, and for my arm they wait.* (Isaiah 51:4–5)

> *The Rock, his work is perfect, for all his ways are justice. A God of faithfulness and without iniquity, just and upright is he.* (Deuteronomy 32:4)

- Wrath.
  - God intensely hates all evil.

  > *The boastful shall not stand before your eyes; you hate all evildoers. You destroy those who speak lies; the Lord abhors the bloodthirsty and deceitful man.* (Psalm 5:5-6)

  > *Since, therefore, we have now been justified by his blood, much more shall we be saved by him from the wrath of God.* (Romans 5:9)

- Jealousy.
  - God is deeply committed to his glory and the good of his people.

  > *For you shall worship no other god, for the LORD, whose name is Jealous, is a jealous God.* (Exodus 34:14)

Humanity experiences relationship **with God.**

> *Thus the LORD used to speak to Moses face to face, as a man speaks to his friend. When Moses turned again into the camp, his assistant Joshua the son of Nun, a young man, would not depart from the tent.* (Exodus 33:11)

> *No longer do I call you servants, for the servant does not know what his master is doing; but I have called you friends, for all that I have heard from my Father I have made known to you.* (John 15:15)

"You have made us for Yourself, O Lord, and our hearts are restless until they rest in You." – Augustine[15]

Humanity is responsible for representing God.

- The Cultural Mandate: Humanity is _____ for stewarding all of God's creation.

> And God blessed them. And God said to them, "Be fruitful and multiply and fill the earth and subdue it, and have dominion over the fish of the sea and over the birds of the heavens and over every living thing that moves on the earth." And God said, "Behold, I have given you every plant yielding seed that is on the face of all the earth, and every tree with seed in its fruit. You shall have them for food. And to every beast of the earth and to every bird of the heavens and to everything that creeps on the earth, everything that has the breath of life, I have given every green plant for food." And it was so. And God saw everything that he had made, and behold, it was very good. And there was evening and there was morning, the sixth day. (Genesis 1:28–31)

  - Ruling in a way that reflects God's goodness.
  - Living in a way that is right for all people.

  > Thus says the LORD: Do justice and righteousness, and deliver from the hand of the oppressor him who has been robbed. And do no wrong or violence to the resident alien, the fatherless, and the widow, nor shed innocent blood in this place. (Jeremiah 22:3)

  > He has told you, O man, what is good; and what does the LORD require of you but to do justice, and to love kindness, and to walk humbly with your God? (Micah 6:8)

- The Great Commission: Humanity is responsible for _____ God's glory to all of the nations.

> And Jesus came and said to them, "All authority in heaven and on earth has been given to me. Go therefore and make disciples

of all nations, baptizing them in the name of the Father and of the Son and of the Holy Spirit, teaching them to observe all that I have commanded you. And behold, I am with you always, to the end of the age." (Matthew 28:18–20)

I am a man or a woman . . .

As image bearers of God, men and women possess equal dignity before God and each other.

So God created man in his own image, in the image of God he created him; male and female he created them. (Genesis 1:27)

As image bearers of God, men and women are uniquely _____ by God in relation to each other.

The man gave names to all livestock and to the birds of the heavens and to every beast of the field. But for Adam there was not found a helper fit for him. So the Lord God caused a deep sleep to fall upon the man, and while he slept took one of his ribs and closed up its place with flesh. And the rib that the Lord God had taken from the man he made into a woman and brought her to the man. Then the man said, "This at last is bone of my bones and flesh of my flesh; she shall be called Woman, because she was taken out of Man." Therefore a man shall leave his father and his mother and hold fast to his wife, and they shall become one flesh. And the man and his wife were both naked and were not ashamed. (Genesis 2:20–25)

- This distinction is divinely designed, not humanly constructed.
  - Gender identity is not chosen by people.
  - Gender identity is given by God.

    "Being created in the image of God and being male or female are essential to being human. Sex (male and female) is not simply biological or genetic, just as being human is not simply biological or genetic. Sex is first and foremost a spiritual and ontological reality created by God. Being male or female cannot be changed by human hands; sex is a category of God's handiwork—his original and everlasting design." – Christopher Yuan[16]

"Transgenderism is not exclusively a battle for what is male and female, but rather a battle for what is true and real. Christians cannot simply nod and smile politely in the face of damaging lies." – Christopher Yuan[17]

○ Gender distinctions are for the flourishing of humanity.
○ Gender distinctions are for the glory of God.

> *"Food is meant for the stomach and the stomach for food"—and God will destroy both one and the other. The body is not meant for sexual immorality, but for the Lord, and the Lord for the body. And God raised the Lord and will also raise us up by his power. Do you not know that your bodies are members of Christ? Shall I then take the members of Christ and make them members of a prostitute? Never! Or do you not know that he who is joined to a prostitute becomes one body with her? For, as it is written, "The two will become one flesh." But he who is joined to the Lord becomes one spirit with him. Flee from sexual immorality. Every other sin a person commits is outside the body, but the sexually immoral person sins against his own body. Or do you not know that your body is a temple of the Holy Spirit within you, whom you have from God? You are not your own, for you were bought with a price. So glorify God in your body. (1 Corinthians 6:13–20)*

• This distinction is _____ expressed in different ways.

> *I praise you, for I am fearfully and wonderfully made. Wonderful are your works; my soul knows it very well. (Psalm 139:14)*

○ Among women . . .

> *So he went and took them and brought them to his mother, and his mother prepared delicious food, such as his father loved. (Genesis 27:14)*

Now Deborah, a prophetess, the wife of Lappidoth, was judging Israel at that time. She used to sit under the palm of Deborah between Ramah and Bethel in the hill country of Ephraim, and the people of Israel came up to her for judgment. She sent and summoned Barak the son of Abinoam from Kedesh-naphtali and said to him, "Has not the LORD, the God of Israel, commanded you, 'Go, gather your men at Mount Tabor, taking 10,000 from the people of Naphtali and the people of Zebulun.'" (Judges 4:4–6)

An excellent wife who can find? She is far more precious than jewels. The heart of her husband trusts in her, and he will have no lack of gain. She does him good, and not harm, all the days of her life. She seeks wool and flax, and works with willing hands. She is like the ships of the merchant; she brings her food from afar. She rises while it is yet night and provides food for her household and portions for her maidens. She considers a field and buys it; with the fruit of her hands she plants a vineyard. She dresses herself with strength and makes her arms strong. She perceives that her merchandise is profitable. Her lamp does not go out at night. She puts her hands to the distaff, and her hands hold the spindle. She opens her hand to the poor and reaches out her hands to the needy. She is not afraid of snow for her household, for all her household are clothed in scarlet. She makes bed coverings for herself; her clothing is fine linen and purple. Her husband is known in the gates when he sits among the elders of the land. She makes linen garments and sells them; she delivers sashes to the merchant. Strength and dignity are her clothing, and she laughs at the time to come. She opens her mouth with wisdom, and the teaching of kindness is on her tongue. She looks well to the ways of her household and does not eat the bread of idleness. Her children rise up and call her blessed; her husband also, and he praises her: "Many women have done excellently, but you surpass them all." Charm is deceitful, and beauty is vain, but a woman who fears the LORD is to be praised. Give her of the fruit of her hands, and let her works praise her in the gates. (Proverbs 31:10–31)

Now there was in Joppa a disciple named Tabitha, which, translated, means Dorcas. She was full of good works and acts of charity. In those days she became ill and died, and when they had washed her, they laid her in an upper room. Since Lydda was near Joppa, the disciples, hearing that Peter was there, sent two men to him, urging him, "Please come to us without delay." So Peter rose and went with them. And when he arrived, they took him to the upper room. All the widows stood beside him weeping and showing tunics and other garments that Dorcas made while she was with them. (Acts 9:36–39)

○ Among men . . .

The man who is the most tender and refined among you will begrudge food to his brother, to the wife he embraces, and to the last of the children whom he has left . . . (Deuteronomy 28:54)

One of the young men answered, "Behold, I have seen a son of Jesse the Bethlehemite, who is skillful in playing, a man of valor, a man of war, prudent in speech, and a man of good presence, and the Lord is with him." (1 Samuel 16:18)

• This distinction is _culturally_ expressed in different ways.

Then I asked her, "Whose daughter are you?" She said, "The daughter of Bethuel, Nahor's son, whom Milcah bore to him." So I put the ring on her nose and the bracelets on her arms. (Genesis 24:47)

I will greatly rejoice in the LORD; my soul shall exult in my God, for he has clothed me with the garments of salvation; he has covered me with the robe of righteousness, as a bridegroom decks himself like a priest with a beautiful headdress, and as a bride adorns herself with her jewels. (Isaiah 61:10)

Any uncircumcised male who is not circumcised in the flesh of his foreskin shall be cut off from his people; he has broken my covenant. (Genesis 17:14)

A woman shall not wear a man's garment, nor shall a man put on a woman's cloak, for whoever does these things is an abomination to the LORD your God. (Deuteronomy 22:5)

Every man who prays or prophesies with his head covered dishonors his head, but every wife who prays or prophesies with her head uncovered dishonors her head, since it is the same as if her head were shaven. (1 Corinthians 11:4–5)

. . . likewise also that women should adorn themselves in respectable apparel, with modesty and self-control, not with braided hair and gold or pearls or costly attire, but with what is proper for women who profess godliness—with good works. (1 Timothy 2:9–10)

- This distinction is particularly expressed in the _____ relationship.

Therefore a man shall leave his father and his mother and hold fast to his wife, and they shall become one flesh. And the man and his wife were both naked and were not ashamed. (Genesis 2:24–25)

  ○ As a picture of how Jesus relates to his church, a husband possesses . . .

  Wives, submit to your own husbands, as to the Lord. For the husband is the head of the wife even as Christ is the head of the church, his body, and is himself its Savior. Now as the church submits to Christ, so also wives should submit in everything to their husbands. Husbands, love your wives, as Christ loved the church and gave himself up for her, that he might sanctify her, having cleansed her by the washing of water with the word, so that he might present the church to himself in splendor, without spot or wrinkle or any such thing, that she might be holy and without blemish. In the same way husbands should love their wives as their own bodies. He who loves his wife loves himself. For no one ever hated his own flesh, but nourishes and cherishes it, just as Christ does the church, because we are members of his body. "Therefore a man shall leave his father and mother and hold fast to his wife, and the two shall become one flesh." This mystery is profound, and I am saying that it refers to Christ and the church. However, let each one of you love his wife as himself, and let the wife see that she respects her husband. (Ephesians 5:22–33)

- Humble authority to lead his family lovingly.
- Sober responsibility to serve his family sacrificially.
- Divine accountability to care for his family faithfully.

○ As a picture of how the church relates to Jesus, a wife . . .

Wives, submit to your husbands, as is fitting in the Lord. Husbands, love your wives, and do not be harsh with them. (Colossians 3:18–19)

Older men are to be sober-minded, dignified, self-controlled, sound in faith, in love, and in steadfastness. Older women likewise are to be reverent in behavior, not slanderers or slaves to much wine. They are to teach what is good, and so train the young women to love their husbands and children, to be self-controlled, pure, working at home, kind, and submissive to their own husbands, that the word of God may not be reviled. (Titus 2:2–5)

Likewise, wives, be subject to your own husbands, so that even if some do not obey the word, they may be won without a word by the conduct of their wives, when they see your respectful and pure conduct. Do not let your adorning be external—the braiding of hair and the putting on of gold jewelry, or the clothing you wear—but let your adorning be the hidden person of the heart with the imperishable beauty of a gentle and quiet spirit, which in God's sight is very precious. For this is how the holy women who hoped in God used to adorn themselves, by submitting to their own husbands, as Sarah obeyed Abraham, calling him lord. And you are her children, if you do good and do not fear anything that is frightening. Likewise, husbands, live with your wives in an understanding way, showing honor to the woman as the weaker vessel, since they are heirs with you of the grace of life, so that your prayers may not be hindered. (1 Peter 3:1–7)

- Supports her husband's oversight of their family.
- Submits to her husband's loving leadership in their family.
- Respects her husband with ultimate reverence for Jesus.

○ A husband and wife's respective roles in marriage . . .
- Arise from God's wisdom, not cultural trends.
- Are grounded in God's good created order, not individual gifting or competency.

And God saw everything that he had made, and behold, it was very good. And there was evening and there was morning, the sixth day. (Genesis 1:31)

WHAT IS WRONG IN THE WORLD?

> **Every human (except for one) has sinned against God, marring the image of God in us, and warranting the judgment of God forever.**

Every human (except for one) has sinned against God . . .

. . . for all have sinned and fall short of the glory of God . . .
(Romans 3:23)

The Definition of Sin . . .

- Sin is any failure to conform to the moral _law_ of God in our attitudes, our actions, or our nature.[18]
  - Our attitudes and actions.

    You shall have no other gods before me. You shall not make for yourself a carved image, or any likeness of anything that is in heaven above, or that is in the earth beneath, or that is in the water under the earth. You shall not bow down to them or serve them, for I the LORD your God am a jealous God, visiting the iniquity of the fathers on the children to the third and the fourth generation of those who hate me, but showing steadfast love to thousands of those who love me and keep my commandments. You shall not take the name of the LORD your God in vain, for the LORD will not hold him guiltless who takes his name in vain. Remember the Sabbath day, to keep it holy. Six days you shall labor, and do all your work, but the seventh day is a Sabbath to the LORD your God. On it you shall not do any work, you, or your son, or your daughter, your male servant, or your female servant, or your livestock, or the sojourner who is within your gates. For in six days the LORD made heaven and earth, the sea, and all that is in them, and rested on the seventh day. Therefore the LORD blessed the Sabbath day and made it holy. Honor your father and your mother, that your days may be long in the land that the LORD your God is giving you. You shall not murder. You shall not commit adultery. You shall not steal. You shall not bear false witness against your neighbor. You shall not covet your neighbor's house; you shall not covet your neighbor's wife, or his male servant, or his female servant, or his ox, or his donkey, or anything that is your neighbor's. (Exodus 20:3–17)

You have heard that it was said to those of old, "You shall not murder; and whoever murders will be liable to judgment." But I say to you that everyone who is angry with his brother will be liable to judgment; whoever insults his brother will be liable to the council; and whoever says, "You fool!" will be liable to the hell of fire. So if you are offering your gift at the altar and there remember that your brother has something against you, leave your gift there before the altar and go. First be reconciled to your brother, and then come and offer your gift. Come to terms quickly with your accuser while you are going with him to court, lest your accuser hand you over to the judge, and the judge to the guard, and you be put in prison. Truly, I say to you, you will never get out until you have paid the last penny. You have heard that it was said, "You shall not commit adultery." But I say to you that everyone who looks at a woman with lustful intent has already committed adultery with her in his heart. If your right eye causes you to sin, tear it out and throw it away. For it is better that you lose one of your members than that your whole body be thrown into hell. And if your right hand causes you to sin, cut it off and throw it away. For it is better that you lose one of your members than that your whole body go into hell. (Matthew 5:21–30)

○ Our nature.

. . . but God shows his love for us in that while we were still sinners, Christ died for us. (Romans 5:8)

. . . among whom we all once lived in the passions of our flesh, carrying out the desires of the body and the mind, and were by nature children of wrath, like the rest of mankind. (Ephesians 2:3)

○ Sin is not (merely) __selfishness__

- Not all self-interest is bad.

  > Say to them, As I live, declares the Lord GOD, I have no
  > pleasure in the death of the wicked, but that the wicked turn
  > from his way and live; turn back, turn back from your evil
  > ways, for why will you die, O house of Israel? (Ezekiel 33:11)

  > . . . but lay up for yourselves treasures in heaven, where
  > neither moth nor rust destroys and where thieves do not
  > break in and steal. (Matthew 6:20)

- Not all selflessness is good.

  > . . . who forbid marriage and require abstinence from foods
  > that God created to be received with thanksgiving by those
  > who believe and know the truth. (1 Timothy 4:3)

  > Let no one disqualify you, insisting on asceticism and worship
  > of angels, going on in detail about visions, puffed up without
  > reason by his sensuous mind . . . These have indeed an
  > appearance of wisdom in promoting self-made religion and
  > asceticism and severity to the body, but they are of no value
  > in stopping the indulgence of the flesh. (Colossians 2:18, 23)

○ Sin is __lawlessness__

> Everyone who makes a practice of sinning also practices lawless-
> ness; sin is lawlessness. (1 John 3:4)

> For all who have sinned without the law will also perish without
> the law, and all who have sinned under the law will be judged
> by the law. For it is not the hearers of the law who are righteous
> before God, but the doers of the law who will be justified. For
> when Gentiles, who do not have the law, by nature do what the
> law requires, they are a law to themselves, even though they do
> not have the law. They show that the work of the law is written on
> their hearts, while their conscience also bears witness, and their
> conflicting thoughts accuse or even excuse them on that day

when, according to my gospel, God judges the secrets of men by Christ Jesus. (Romans 2:12–16)

○ God is not the author of sin.

Therefore, hear me, you men of understanding: far be it from God that he should do wickedness, and from the Almighty that he should do wrong. (Job 34:10)

Let no one say when he is tempted, "I am being tempted by God," for God cannot be tempted with evil, and he himself tempts no one. (James 1:13)

○ God ultimately has authority over sin.

In him we have obtained an inheritance, having been predestined according to the purpose of him who works all things according to the counsel of his will . . . (Ephesians 1:11)

. . . all the inhabitants of the earth are accounted as nothing, and he does according to his will among the host of heaven and among the inhabitants of the earth; and none can stay his hand or say to him, "What have you done?" (Daniel 4:35)

The Anatomy of Sin . . .

Now the serpent was more crafty than any other beast of the field that the LORD God had made. He said to the woman, "Did God actually say, 'You shall not eat of any tree in the garden'?" And the woman said to the serpent, "We may eat of the fruit of the trees in the garden, but God said, 'You shall not eat of the fruit of the tree that is in the midst of the garden, neither shall you touch it, lest you die.'" But the serpent said to the woman, "You will not surely die. For God knows that when you eat of it your eyes will be opened, and you will be like God, knowing good and evil." So when the woman saw that the tree was good for food, and that it was a delight to the eyes, and that the tree was to be desired to make one wise, she took of its fruit and ate, and she also gave some to her husband who was with *her, and he ate. Then the eyes of both were opened, and they knew that they were naked. And they sewed fig leaves together and made themselves loincloths. (Genesis 3:1–7)*

- Sin is rejecting God's Word.
- Sin is spurning God's authority.
- Sin is denying God's character.
- Sin is trying to take God's _place_ .
  - Am I made in the image of God?
  - Or should I try to take the place of God?

- Sin is our attempt to define who we are (establish our identity) and how we live (achieve our destiny) apart from who God is and how God has designed us to live.

The Foolishness of Sin . . .

The way of a fool is right in his own eyes, but a wise man listens to advice. (Proverbs 12:15)

- We transgress the law that is for our _good_ .

And Aaron shall lay both his hands on the head of the live goat, and confess over it all the iniquities of the people of Israel, and all their transgressions, all their sins. And he shall put them on the head of the goat and send it away into the wilderness by the hand of a man who is in readiness. (Leviticus 16:21)

- We turn from the only One who can give us _life_ .

Be appalled, O heavens, at this; be shocked, be utterly desolate, declares the LORD, for my people have committed two evils: they have forsaken me, the fountain of living waters, and hewed out cisterns for themselves, broken cisterns that can hold no water. (Jeremiah 2:12–13)

The Pervasiveness of Sin . . .

The LORD saw that the wickedness of man was great in the earth, and that every intention of the thoughts of his heart was only evil continually. (Genesis 6:5)

- Our nature is sinful from __birth__.

    Behold, I was brought forth in iniquity, and in sin did my mother conceive me. (Psalm 51:5)

- Our minds are blinded.

    And since they did not see fit to acknowledge God, God gave them up to a debased mind to do what ought not to be done. They were filled with all manner of unrighteousness, evil, covetousness, malice. They are full of envy, murder, strife, deceit, maliciousness. They are gossips, slanderers, haters of God, insolent, haughty, boastful, inventors of evil, disobedient to parents, foolish, faithless, heartless, ruthless. Though they know God's righteous decree that those who practice such things deserve to die, they not only do them but give approval to those who practice them. (Romans 1:28–32)

    In their case the god of this world has blinded the minds of the unbelievers, to keep them from seeing the light of the gospel of the glory of Christ, who is the image of God. (2 Corinthians 4:4)

- Our desires are disordered.

    For this reason God gave them up to dishonorable passions. For their women exchanged natural relations for those that are contrary to nature; and the men likewise gave up natural relations with women and were consumed with passion for one another, men committing shameless acts with men and receiving in themselves the due penalty for their error. (Romans 1:26–27)

    Beloved, I urge you as sojourners and exiles to abstain from the passions of the flesh, which wage war against your soul. (1 Peter 2:11)

- Our bodies are defiled.

> *Therefore God gave them up in the lusts of their hearts to impurity, to the dishonoring of their bodies among themselves, because they exchanged the truth about God for a lie and worshiped and served the creature rather than the Creator, who is blessed forever! Amen.* (Romans 1:24–25)

> *Their throat is an open grave; they use their tongues to deceive. The venom of asps is under their lips. Their mouth is full of curses and bitterness. Their feet are swift to shed blood; in their paths are ruin and misery, and the way of peace they have not known. There is no fear of God before their eyes.* (Romans 3:13–18)

- Our wills are distorted.

> *. . . as it is written: "None is righteous, no, not one; no one understands; no one seeks for God. All have turned aside; together they have become worthless; no one does good, not even one."* (Romans 3:10–12)

> *For the mind that is set on the flesh is hostile to God, for it does not submit to God's law; indeed, it cannot.* (Romans 8:7)

- Our relationships are __broken__.
  - With God.

> *And they heard the sound of the LORD God walking in the garden in the cool of the day, and the man and his wife hid themselves from the presence of the LORD God among the trees of the garden. But the LORD God called to the man and said to him, "Where are you?" And he said, "I heard the sound of you in the garden, and I was afraid, because I was naked, and I hid myself."* (Genesis 3:8–10)

> *You adulterous people! Do you not know that friendship with the world is enmity with God? Therefore whoever wishes to be a friend of the world makes himself an enemy of God.* (James 4:4)

○ With one another.

> *Cain spoke to Abel his brother. And when they were in the field, Cain rose up against his brother Abel and killed him. (Genesis 4:8)*

> *For we ourselves were once foolish, disobedient, led astray, slaves to various passions and pleasures, passing our days in malice and envy, hated by others and hating one another. (Titus 3:3)*

. . . marring the image of God in us . . .

The image of God maintained: we are ___still___ like God.

> *Whoever sheds the blood of man, by man shall his blood be shed, for God made man in his own image. (Genesis 9:6)*

> *With it we bless our Lord and Father, and with it we curse people who are made in the likeness of God. (James 3:9)*

The image of God distorted: we are ___less___ like God.

> *See, this alone I found, that God made man upright, but they have sought out many schemes. (Ecclesiastes 7:29)*

> "We must state both that after his revolt mankind remains mankind, and also that mankind has radically changed, that he is but a grisly shadow of himself. Mankind remains the image of God, inviolable and responsible, but has become a contradictory image, one might say a caricature, a witness against himself." – Henri Blocher[19]

. . . and warranting the judgment of God forever.

For the wages of sin is death, but the free gift of God is eternal life in Christ Jesus our Lord. (Romans 6:23)

We _deserve_ condemnation in a just, eternal, horrifying hell.

And if your hand causes you to sin, cut it off. It is better for you to enter life crippled than with two hands to go to hell, to the unquenchable fire. And if your foot causes you to sin, cut it off. It is better for you to enter life lame than with two feet to be thrown into hell. And if your eye causes you to sin, tear it out. It is better for you to enter the kingdom of God with one eye than with two eyes to be thrown into hell, "where their worm does not die and the fire is not quenched." For everyone will be salted with fire. Salt is good, but if the salt has lost its saltiness, how will you make it salty again? Have salt in yourselves, and be at peace with one another. (Mark 9:43–48)

Then I saw a great white throne and him who was seated on it. From his presence earth and sky fled away, and no place was found for them. And I saw the dead, great and small, standing before the throne, and books were opened. Then another book was opened, which is the book of life. And the dead were judged by what was written in the books, according to what they had done. And the sea gave up the dead who were in it, Death and Hades gave up the dead who were in them, and they were judged, each one of them, according to what they had done. Then Death and Hades were thrown into the lake of fire. This is the second death, the lake of fire. And if anyone's name was not found written in the book of life, he was thrown into the lake of fire. (Revelation 20:11–15)

HOW CAN IT BE MADE RIGHT?
HOW CAN I (HOW CAN WE) EXPERIENCE THE GOOD LIFE?

What We Don't Need . . .

- Sinners practicing superficial _before God_

What to me is the multitude of your sacrifices? says the LORD; I have had enough of burnt offerings of rams and the fat of well-fed beasts; I do not delight in the blood of bulls, or of lambs, or of goats. When you come to appear before me, who has required of you this trampling of my courts? Bring no more vain offerings; incense is an abomination to me. New moon and Sabbath and the calling of convocations—I cannot endure iniquity and solemn assembly. Your new moons and your appointed feasts my soul hates; they have become a burden to me; I am weary of bearing them. When you spread out your hands, I will hide my eyes from you; even though you make many prayers, I will not listen; your hands are full of blood. Wash yourselves; make yourselves clean; remove the evil of your deeds from before my eyes; cease to do evil . . . (Isaiah 1:11–16)

- ○ We don't need to try harder to do better.

  The sin of Judah is written with a pen of iron; with a point of diamond it is engraved on the tablet of their heart, and on the horns of their altars . . . (Jeremiah 17:1)

- ○ We don't need attempts to redefine ourselves in our image.

  Therefore God gave them up in the lusts of their hearts to impurity, to the dishonoring of their bodies among themselves, because they exchanged the truth about God for a lie and worshiped and served the creature rather than the Creator, who is blessed forever! Amen. (Romans 1:24–25)

What We Do Need . . .

- A Savior who brings supernatural _regeneration_

> For the Son of Man came to seek and to save the lost. (Luke 19:10)
>
> The thief comes only to steal and kill and destroy. I came that they may have life and have it abundantly. (John 10:10)

- We need a new heart and a new life.

> And I will give you a new heart, and a new spirit I will put within you. And I will remove the heart of stone from your flesh and give you a heart of flesh. And I will put my Spirit within you, and cause you to walk in my statutes and be careful to obey my rules. (Ezekiel 36:26–27)
>
> Jesus answered him, "Truly, truly, I say to you, unless one is born again he cannot see the kingdom of God." (John 3:3)

- We need our Creator to restore our lives in his image.

> . . . to put off your old self, which belongs to your former manner of life and is corrupt through deceitful desires, and to be renewed in the spirit of your minds, and to put on the new self, created after the likeness of God in true righteousness and holiness. (Ephesians 4:22–24)

Our Creator has come!

> Therefore the Lord himself will give you a sign. Behold, the virgin shall conceive and bear a son, and shall call his name Immanuel. (Isaiah 7:14)
>
> "She will bear a son, and you shall call his name Jesus, for he will save his people from their sins." All this took place to fulfill what the Lord had spoken by the prophet: "Behold, the virgin shall conceive and bear a son, and they shall call his name Immanuel" (which means, God with us). (Matthew 1:21–23)

- Jesus is the _perfect human_

> *Have this mind among yourselves, which is yours in Christ Jesus, who, though he was in the form of God, did not count equality with God a thing to be grasped, but emptied himself, by taking the form of a servant, being born in the likeness of men. And being found in human form, he humbled himself by becoming obedient to the point of death, even death on a cross. Therefore God has highly exalted him and bestowed on him the name that is above every name, so that at the name of Jesus every knee should bow, in heaven and on earth and under the earth, and every tongue confess that Jesus Christ is Lord, to the glory of God the Father. (Philippians 2:5–11)*

- Jesus is fully _God_.

> *In the beginning was the Word, and the Word was with God, and the Word was God. He was in the beginning with God. All things were made through him, and without him was not any thing made that was made. In him was life, and the life was the light of men. (John 1:1–4)*

> *Jesus said to them, "Truly, truly, I say to you, before Abraham was, I am." (John 8:58)*

> *I and the Father are one. (John 10:30)*

> *For in him the whole fullness of deity dwells bodily . . . (Colossians 2:9)*

- Jesus is fully _human_.

> *For there is one God, and there is one mediator between God and men, the man Christ Jesus, who gave himself as a ransom for all, which is the testimony given at the proper time. (1 Timothy 2:5–6)*

> *Therefore he had to be made like his brothers in every respect, so that he might become a merciful and faithful high priest in the*

service of God, to make propitiation for the sins of the people.
(Hebrews 2:17)

○ Adam was fully human; Jesus is truly human.

> *He is the image of the invisible God, the firstborn of all creation.*
> (Colossians 1:15)

> *In their case the god of this world has blinded the minds of the unbelievers, to keep them from seeing the light of the gospel of the glory of Christ, who is the image of God.* (2 Corinthians 4:4)

○ He was born of a virgin.

> *Now the birth of Jesus Christ took place in this way. When his mother Mary had been betrothed to Joseph, before they came together she was found to be with child from the Holy Spirit. And her husband Joseph, being a just man and unwilling to put her to shame, resolved to divorce her quietly. But as he considered these things, behold, an angel of the Lord appeared to him in a dream, saying, "Joseph, son of David, do not fear to take Mary as your wife, for that which is conceived in her is from the Holy Spirit."* (Matthew 1:18–20)

> *And the angel answered her, "The Holy Spirit will come upon you, and the power of the Most High will overshadow you; therefore the child to be born will be called holy—the Son of God."* (Luke 1:35)

○ He possessed the full range of human characteristics.
  ▪ A human body.

> *And she gave birth to her firstborn son and wrapped him in swaddling cloths and laid him in a manger, because there was no place for them in the inn.* (Luke 2:7)

> *Jacob's well was there; so Jesus, wearied as he was from his journey, was sitting beside the well. It was about the sixth hour.* (John 4:6)

> *And after fasting forty days and forty nights, he was hungry.*
> *(Matthew 4:2)*

- A human mind.

  > *And Jesus increased in wisdom and in stature and in favor with God and man. (Luke 2:52)*

- A human soul.

  > *Now is my soul troubled. And what shall I say? "Father, save me from this hour"? But for this purpose I have come to this hour. (John 12:27)*

- Human emotions.

  > *When Jesus heard this, he marveled and said to those who followed him, "Truly, I tell you, with no one in Israel have I found such faith." (Matthew 8:10)*

  > *Jesus wept. (John 11:35)*

- Human observation.

  > *And when Jesus had finished these parables, he went away from there, and coming to his hometown he taught them in their synagogue, so that they were astonished, and said, "Where did this man get this wisdom and these mighty works? Is not this the carpenter's son? Is not his mother called Mary? And are not his brothers James and Joseph and Simon and Judas? And are not all his sisters with us? Where then did this man get all these things?" And they took offense at him. But Jesus said to them, "A prophet is not without honor except in his hometown and in his own household." And he did not do many mighty works there, because of their unbelief. (Matthew 13:53–58)*

○ Jesus is fully able to identify with us.

Since then we have a great high priest who has passed through the heavens, Jesus, the Son of God, let us hold fast our confession. For we do not have a high priest who is unable to sympathize with our weaknesses, but one who in every respect has been tempted as we are, yet without sin. Let us then with confidence draw near to the throne of grace, that we may receive mercy and find grace to help in time of need. (Hebrews 4:14–16)

- He is familiar with our struggles.
- He is familiar with our sorrow.
- He is familiar with our suffering.
- Yet he is without sin.

> *He committed no sin, neither was deceit found in his mouth.* (1 Peter 2:22)

- Jesus came to __save__ us from our sin.

> *She will bear a son, and you shall call his name Jesus, for he will save his people from their sins.* (Matthew 1:21)

> *For the Son of Man came to seek and to save the lost.* (Luke 19:10)

  ○ Jesus came to __love__ the life we could not live.

  > *You know that he appeared in order to take away sins, and in him there is no sin.* (1 John 3:5)

  ○ Jesus came to __die__ the death we deserve to die.

  > *. . . but God shows his love for us in that while we were still sinners, Christ died for us.* (Romans 5:8)

    - He assumed our identity.

    > *Therefore he had to be made like his brothers in every respect, so that he might become a merciful and faithful high*

priest in the service of God, to make propitiation for the sins of the people. (Hebrews 2:17)

- He accomplished our salvation.

  And you, who once were alienated and hostile in mind, doing evil deeds, he has now reconciled in his body of flesh by his death, in order to present you holy and blameless and above reproach before him . . . (Colossians 1:21–22)

  ○ Jesus came to ___Conquer___ the enemy we could not conquer.

  For I delivered to you as of first importance what I also received: that Christ died for our sins in accordance with the Scriptures, that he was buried, that he was raised on the third day in accordance with the Scriptures . . . (1 Corinthians 15:3–4)

- We can be transformed more and more into the ___likeness___ of God.

  . . . and have put on the new self, which is being renewed in knowledge after the image of its creator. (Colossians 3:10)

  And we all, with unveiled face, beholding the glory of the Lord, are being transformed into the same image from one degree of glory to another. For this comes from the Lord who is the Spirit. (2 Corinthians 3:18)

New creation is possible!

- New ___birth___ . . .

  Jesus answered, "Truly, truly, I say to you, unless one is born of water and the Spirit, he cannot enter the kingdom of God. That which is born of the flesh is flesh, and that which is born of the Spirit is spirit. Do not marvel that I said to you, 'You must be born again.' The wind blows where it wishes, and you hear its sound, but you do not know where it comes from or where it goes. So it is with everyone who is born of the Spirit." (John 3:5–8)

- By God's grace, we turn from our sin and ourselves.

  And Peter said to them, "Repent and be baptized every one of you in the name of Jesus Christ for the forgiveness of your sins, and you will receive the gift of the Holy Spirit." (Acts 2:38)

  Repent therefore, and turn back, that your sins may be blotted out . . . (Acts 3:19)

- By God's grace, we trust in Jesus as Savior and Lord.

  Let all the house of Israel therefore know for certain that God has made him both Lord and Christ, this Jesus whom you crucified. (Acts 2:36)

  And they said, "Believe in the Lord Jesus, and you will be saved, you and your household." (Acts 16:31)

- The way to happiness is not through _Adam_ . . .
  - Rejecting God's Word.
  - Spurning God's authority.
  - Denying God's character.
  - Trying to take God's place.

- The way to happiness is through _Jesus_ . . .
  - Receiving God's Word.

  But to all who did receive him, who believed in his name, he gave the right to become children of God, who were born, not of blood nor of the will of the flesh nor of the will of man, but of God. (John 1:12–13)

  . . . since you have been born again, not of perishable seed but of imperishable, through the living and abiding word of God . . . (1 Peter 1:23)

○ Submitting to God's authority.

> . . . because, if you confess with your mouth that Jesus is Lord and believe in your heart that God raised him from the dead, you will be saved. (Romans 10:9)

○ Trusting God's character.

> For God so loved the world, that he gave his only Son, that whoever believes in him should not perish but have eternal life. (John 3:16)

○ Living in God's image.

> Therefore, if anyone is in Christ, he is a new creation. The old has passed away; behold, the new has come. (2 Corinthians 5:17)

- New _Identity_ . . .

> But if, in our endeavor to be justified in Christ, we too were found to be sinners, is Christ then a servant of sin? Certainly not! For if I rebuild what I tore down, I prove myself to be a transgressor. For through the law I died to the law, so that I might live to God. I have been crucified with Christ. It is no longer I who live, but Christ who lives in me. And the life I now live in the flesh I live by faith in the Son of God, who loved me and gave himself for me. I do not nullify the grace of God, for if righteousness were through the law, then Christ died for no purpose. (Galatians 2:17–21)

"Simply put, Christians should have a positive view of themselves—in Christ. As the secular world lies in the sun of ignorance and licks itself with self-help gurus cheaply affirming their self-worth, the born-again Christian should have the most concrete, positive, confident self-image on the planet. Not because he is sinless. Not because he wakes up every morning and reads his Bible. Not because he is more selfless than his fellow man. But because God has made him alive, forgiven him all of his trespasses, adopted him into his family, and dwells in him. If any man desires true self-worth, he should

see all he can hope for in the shining faces of the church of God."
– Greg Morse[20]

- Jesus is in us, we are in Jesus, we are with Jesus, and Jesus is with us.
- Jesus is __in__ us.

> To them God chose to make known how great among the Gentiles are the riches of the glory of this mystery, which is Christ in you, the hope of glory. (Colossians 1:27)

- Jesus died for you so that he might live in you.

> "Oh, it is joy to feel Jesus living in you; to find your heart all taken up by Him; to be reminded of His love by *His* seeking communion with you at all times, not by your painful attempts to abide in Him. He is our life, our strength, our salvation. . . . I am no longer anxious about anything . . . for He, I know, is able to carry out His will, and His will is mine. It makes no matter where He places me, or how. That is rather for Him to consider than for me; for in the easiest position He must give me His grace, and in the most difficult His grace is sufficient. So if God should place me in great perplexity, must He not give me much guidance; in positions of great difficulty, much grace; in circumstances of great pressure and trial, much strength. I have no fear that His resources will be unequal to the emergency! And His resources are mine—for He is mine, and is with me and dwells in me."
> – Hudson Taylor[21]

- Christ in you now means Christ in you forever.

> When Christ who is your life appears, then you also will appear with him in glory. (Colossians 3:4)

- We are __in__ Jesus.

> Therefore, if anyone is in Christ, he is a new creation. The old has passed away; behold, the new has come. (2 Corinthians 5:17)

And the peace of God, which surpasses all understanding, will guard your hearts and your minds in Christ Jesus. (Philippians 4:7)

○ We are _with_ Jesus.

Now if we have died with Christ, we believe that we will also live with him. (Romans 6:8)

For if we have been united with him in a death like his, we shall certainly be united with him in a resurrection like his. (Romans 6:5)

But God, being rich in mercy, because of the great love with which he loved us, even when we were dead in our trespasses, made us alive together with Christ—by grace you have been saved—and raised us up with him and seated us with him in the heavenly places in Christ Jesus, so that in the coming ages he might show the immeasurable riches of his grace in kindness toward us in Christ Jesus. (Ephesians 2:4–7)

○ Jesus is _with_ us.

The grace of the Lord Jesus be with you. (1 Corinthians 16:23)

Now may the Lord of peace himself give you peace at all times in every way. The Lord be with you all. I, Paul, write this greeting with my own hand. This is the sign of genuineness in every letter of mine; it is the way I write. The grace of our Lord Jesus Christ be with you all. (2 Thessalonians 3:16–18)

. . . teaching them to observe all that I have commanded you. And behold, I am with you always, to the end of the age. (Matthew 28:20)

○ A _spiritual_ identity.
  ▪ We are in the Father.

I do not ask for these only, but also for those who will believe in me through their word, that they may all be one, just as you, Father, are in me, and I in you, that they also may be in us, so that the world may believe that you have sent me. (John 17:20–21)

- We are in the Holy Spirit.

    You, however, are not in the flesh but in the Spirit, if in fact the Spirit of God dwells in you. Anyone who does not have the Spirit of Christ does not belong to him. (Romans 8:9)

- The Father is in us.

    Jesus answered him, "If anyone loves me, he will keep my word, and my Father will love him, and we will come to him and make our home with him." (John 14:23)

- The Holy Spirit is in us.

    Do you not know that you are God's temple and that God's Spirit dwells in you? (1 Corinthians 3:16)

- We have fellowship with the Father.

    . . . that which we have seen and heard we proclaim also to you, so that you too may have fellowship with us; and indeed our fellowship is with the Father and with his Son Jesus Christ. (1 John 1:3)

- We have fellowship with the Holy Spirit.

    The grace of the Lord Jesus Christ and the love of God and the fellowship of the Holy Spirit be with you all. (2 Corinthians 13:14)

○ A spiritual identity.

But he who is joined to the Lord becomes one spirit with him.
(1 Corinthians 6:17)

You, however, are not in the flesh but in the Spirit, if in fact the Spirit of God dwells in you. Anyone who does not have the Spirit of Christ does not belong to him. But if Christ is in you, although the body is dead because of sin, the Spirit is life because of righteousness. If the Spirit of him who raised Jesus from the dead dwells in you, he who raised Christ Jesus from the dead will also give life to your mortal bodies through his Spirit who dwells in you. (Romans 8:9–11)

"We must now examine this question. How do we receive those benefits which the Father bestowed on his only-begotten Son—not for Christ's own private use, but that he might enrich poor and needy men? First, we must understand that as long as Christ remains outside of us, and we are separated from him, all that he has suffered and done for the salvation of the human race remains useless and of no value for us. . . . [A]ll that he possesses is nothing to us until we grow into one body with him. . . . [T]he Holy Spirit is the bond by which Christ effectually unites us to himself." – John Calvin[22]

○ A deep identity.

For no one ever hated his own flesh, but nourishes and cherishes it, just as Christ does the church, because we are members of his body. "Therefore a man shall leave his father and mother and hold fast to his wife, and the two shall become one flesh." This mystery is profound, and I am saying that it refers to Christ and the church. However, let each one of you love his wife as himself, and let the wife see that she respects her husband. (Ephesians 5:29–32)

○ A vital identity.

So you also must consider yourselves dead to sin and alive to God in Christ Jesus. (Romans 6:11)

> *For to me to live is Christ, and to die is gain.* (Philippians 1:21)

○ A personal identity.

> *Indeed, I count everything as loss because of the surpassing worth of knowing Christ Jesus my Lord. For his sake I have suffered the loss of all things and count them as rubbish, in order that I may gain Christ and be found in him, not having a righteousness of my own that comes from the law, but that which comes through faith in Christ, the righteousness from God that depends on faith—that I may know him and the power of his resurrection, and may share his sufferings, becoming like him in his death, that by any means possible I may attain the resurrection from the dead.* (Philippians 3:8–11)

○ A _____ identity.

> *There is neither Jew nor Greek, there is neither slave nor free, there is no male and female, for you are all one in Christ Jesus.* (Galatians 3:28)

> *But when the fullness of time had come, God sent forth his Son, born of woman, born under the law, to redeem those who were under the law, so that we might receive adoption as sons. And because you are sons, God has sent the Spirit of his Son into our hearts, crying, "Abba! Father!" So you are no longer a slave, but a son, and if a son, then an heir through God. Formerly, when you did not know God, you were enslaved to those that by nature are not gods.* (Galatians 4:4–8)

> *For through him we both have access in one Spirit to the Father. So then you are no longer strangers and aliens, but you are fellow citizens with the saints and members of the household of God, built on the foundation of the apostles and prophets, Christ Jesus himself being the cornerstone, in whom the whole structure, being joined together, grows into a holy temple in the Lord. In him you also are being built together into a dwelling place for God by the Spirit.* (Ephesians 2:18–22)

- God calls men and women his sons and daughters.

> "So it is with the family of God. Republican or Democrat, liberal or conservative, we are first, foremost, and always sons and daughters of the same Father. Made in his image, we are called now to bear it—to embody and express the reality of God our Father in all spheres of life, including politics. Sadly, many Christians today bear the image of their preferred political leader or tribe more proudly and clearly than the image of their Father. Their identity is more profoundly shaped by a worldly god than the transcendent God. As a result, observers often can't look at an assortment of Christians and say, 'I see their family resemblance' Because while many Christians might bear the name of Christ, it isn't clear that they bear his image as their truest source of identity and allegiance."
> — Julius Kim[23]

- They are co-heirs in his kingdom.
- They are co-laborers in his mission.
- They relate to one another as siblings, not as subordinates.

> *Do not rebuke an older man but encourage him as you would a father, younger men as brothers, older women as mothers, younger women as sisters, in all purity.*
> (1 Timothy 5:1–2)

- God gives men and women spiritual gifts.

> *Now there are varieties of gifts, but the same Spirit; and there are varieties of service, but the same Lord; and there are varieties of activities, but it is the same God who empowers them all in everyone. To each is given the manifestation of the Spirit for the common good. For to one is given through the Spirit the utterance of wisdom, and to another the utterance of knowledge according to the same Spirit, to another faith by the same Spirit, to another gifts of healing by the one Spirit, to another the working of miracles, to another*

prophecy, to another the ability to distinguish between spirits, to another various kinds of tongues, to another the interpretation of tongues. All these are empowered by one and the same Spirit, who apportions to each one individually as he wills. For just as the body is one and has many members, and all the members of the body, though many, are one body, so it is with Christ. For in one Spirit we were all baptized into one body—Jews or Greeks, slaves or free—and all were made to drink of one Spirit. (1 Corinthians 12:4–13)

- For the building up of his church.
- For the spread of the gospel.
- The contribution of both men and women serving in the church is vital to the health of the church.
- The church is incomplete without a full complement of men and women partnering together in ministry, using all of their gifts according to God's good design for God's great glory.

> Greet Prisca and Aquila, my fellow workers in Christ Jesus, who risked their necks for my life, to whom not only I give thanks but all the churches of the Gentiles give thanks as well. Greet also the church in their house. Greet my beloved Epaenetus, who was the first convert to Christ in Asia. Greet Mary, who has worked hard for you. Greet Andronicus and Junia, my kinsmen and my fellow prisoners. They are well known to the apostles, and they were in Christ before me. Greet Ampliatus, my beloved in the Lord. Greet Urbanus, our fellow worker in Christ, and my beloved Stachys. Greet Apelles, who is approved in Christ. Greet those who belong to the family of Aristobulus. Greet my kinsman Herodion. Greet those in the Lord who belong to the family of Narcissus. Greet those workers in the Lord, Tryphaena and Tryphosa. Greet the beloved Persis, who has worked hard in the Lord. Greet Rufus, chosen in the Lord; also his mother, who has been a mother to me as well. Greet Asyncritus, Phlegon, Hermes, Patrobas, Hermas, and the brothers

> who are with them. Greet Philologus, Julia, Nereus and his sister, and Olympas, and all the saints who are with them. (Romans 16:3–15)

○ An _____ identity.
  ▪ From eternity past . . .

> Blessed be the God and Father of our Lord Jesus Christ, who has blessed us in Christ with every spiritual blessing in the heavenly places, even as he chose us in him before the foundation of the world, that we should be holy and blameless before him. . . . (Ephesians 1:3–4)

  ▪ To eternity future.

> And we know that for those who love God all things work together for good, for those who are called according to his purpose. For those whom he foreknew he also predestined to be conformed to the image of his Son, in order that he might be the firstborn among many brothers. And those whom he predestined he also called, and those whom he called he also justified, and those whom he justified he also glorified. What then shall we say to these things? If God is for us, who can be against us? He who did not spare his own Son but gave him up for us all, how will he not also with him graciously give us all things? Who shall bring any charge against God's elect? It is God who justifies. Who is to condemn? Christ Jesus is the one who died—more than that, who was raised—who is at the right hand of God, who indeed is interceding for us. Who shall separate us from the love of Christ? Shall tribulation, or distress, or persecution, or famine, or nakedness, or danger, or sword? As it is written, "For your sake we are being killed all the day long; we are regarded as sheep to be slaughtered." No, in all these things we are more than conquerors through him who loved us. For I am sure that neither death nor life, nor angels nor rulers, nor things present nor things to come, nor powers, nor height nor depth, nor anything else in all creation, will be able to

separate us from the love of God in Christ Jesus our Lord.
(Romans 8:28–39)

- A new _image_ ...

> And we all, with unveiled face, beholding the glory of the Lord,
> are being transformed into the same image from one degree of
> glory to another. For this comes from the Lord who is the Spirit.
> (2 Corinthians 3:18)

> "It is the will of God to have the Spirit of God use the Word of
> God to make the children of God look like the Son of God."
> – H.B. Charles[24]

  - All who trust in Jesus are being conformed to the image of Jesus.

    > His divine power has granted to us all things that pertain to life
    > and godliness, through the knowledge of him who called us to
    > his own glory and excellence, by which he has granted to us his
    > precious and very great promises, so that through them you
    > may become partakers of the divine nature, having escaped
    > from the corruption that is in the world because of sinful desire.
    > (2 Peter 1:3–4)

  - A daily struggle.

    > But I say, walk by the Spirit, and you will not gratify the desires
    > of the flesh. For the desires of the flesh are against the Spirit,
    > and the desires of the Spirit are against the flesh, for these are
    > opposed to each other, to keep you from doing the things you
    > want to do. But if you are led by the Spirit, you are not under the
    > law. (Galatians 5:16–18)

    - Mortification of the flesh (sarx).

      > Now the works of the flesh are evident: sexual immorality,
      > impurity, sensuality, idolatry, sorcery, enmity, strife, jealousy,
      > fits of anger, rivalries, dissensions, divisions, envy,
      > drunkenness, orgies, and things like these. I warn you, as I

warned you before, that those who do such things will not inherit the kingdom of God. (Galatians 5:19–21)

- Vivification of the spirit (*pneuma*).

    But the fruit of the Spirit is love, joy, peace, patience, kindness, goodness, faithfulness, gentleness, self-control; against such things there is no law. And those who belong to Christ Jesus have crucified the flesh with its passions and desires. If we live by the Spirit, let us also keep in step with the Spirit. (Galatians 5:22–25)

○ A _gradual_ transformation.

Therefore, my beloved, as you have always obeyed, so now, not only as in my presence but much more in my absence, work out your own salvation with fear and trembling, for it is God who works in you, both to will and to work for his good pleasure. (Philippians 2:12–13)

- He is transforming our minds.

    I appeal to you therefore, brothers, by the mercies of God, to present your bodies as a living sacrifice, holy and acceptable to God, which is your spiritual worship. Do not be conformed to this world, but be transformed by the renewal of your mind, that by testing you may discern what is the will of God, what is good and acceptable and perfect. (Romans 12:1–2)

- He is transforming our desires.

    Beloved, I urge you as sojourners and exiles to abstain from the passions of the flesh, which wage war against your soul. (1 Peter 2:11)

    Do not love the world or the things in the world. If anyone loves the world, the love of the Father is not in him. (1 John 2:15)

- He is transforming our wills.

> Therefore, my beloved, as you have always obeyed, so now, not only as in my presence but much more in my absence, work out your own salvation with fear and trembling, for it is God who works in you, both to will and to work for his good pleasure. (Philippians 2:12–13)

- He is transforming our bodies.

> What agreement has the temple of God with idols? For we are the temple of the living God; as God said, "I will make my dwelling among them and walk among them, and I will be their God, and they shall be my people. Therefore go out from their midst, and be separate from them, says the Lord, and touch no unclean thing; then I will welcome you, and I will be a father to you, and you shall be sons and daughters to me, says the Lord Almighty." Since we have these promises, beloved, let us cleanse ourselves from every defilement of body and spirit, bringing holiness to completion in the fear of God. (2 Corinthians 6:16–7:1)

- He is transforming our _relationships_
  - In the church.

> By this all people will know that you are my disciples, if you have love for one another. (John 13:35)

  - In the world.

> And Jesus came and said to them, "All authority in heaven and on earth has been given to me. Go therefore and make disciples of all nations, baptizing them in the name of the Father and of the Son and of the Holy Spirit, teaching them to observe all that I have commanded you. And behold, I am with you always, to the end of the age." (Matthew 28:18–20)

- This process of transformation will __not__ be complete in this world.

> If we say we have no sin, we deceive ourselves, and the truth is not in us. If we confess our sins, he is faithful and just to forgive us our sins and to cleanse us from all unrighteousness. If we say we have not sinned, we make him a liar, and his word is not in us. (1 John 1:8–10)

> "Indeed, the more sanctified the person is, the more conformed he is to the image of his Savior, the more he must recoil against every lack of conformity to the holiness of God. The deeper his apprehension of the majesty of God, the greater the intensity of his love to God, the more persistent his yearning for the attainment of the prize of the high calling of God in Christ Jesus, the more conscious will he be of the gravity of the sin that remains and the more poignant will be his detestation of it. . . . Was this not the effect in all the people of God as they came into closer proximity to the revelation of God's holiness?" – John Murray[25]

- This is not an excuse for spiritual laziness.
- This is an exhortation to spiritual perseverance.

> Here is a call for the endurance of the saints, those who keep the commandments of God and their faith in Jesus. (Revelation 14:12)

- This process of transformation __will__ be complete in the world to come.

> Beloved, we are God's children now, and what we will be has not yet appeared; but we know that when he appears we shall be like him, because we shall see him as he is. And everyone who thus hopes in him purifies himself as he is pure. (1 John 3:2–3)

- In Adam, we are fully human.
- In Jesus, we are becoming—and will become!— _truly_ human.

As long as we remain in this world, the good life involves doing and promoting justice and righteousness as a _____ of the God in whose image we are made.

> *And God blessed them. And God said to them, "Be fruitful and multiply and fill the earth and subdue it, and have dominion over the fish of the sea and over the birds of the heavens and over every living thing that moves on the earth." And God said, "Behold, I have given you every plant yielding seed that is on the face of all the earth, and every tree with seed in its fruit. You shall have them for food. And to every beast of the earth and to every bird of the heavens and to everything that creeps on the earth, everything that has the breath of life, I have given every green plant for food." And it was so. And God saw everything that he had made, and behold, it was very good. And there was evening and there was morning, the sixth day. (Genesis 1:28–31)*

> *Yet you have made him a little lower than the heavenly beings and crowned him with glory and honor. You have given him dominion over the works of your hands; you have put all things under his feet, all sheep and oxen, and also the beasts of the field, the birds of the heavens, and the fish of the sea, whatever passes along the paths of the seas. (Psalm 8:5–8)*

> *He has told you, O man, what is good; and what does the LORD require of you but to do justice, and to love kindness, and to walk humbly with your God? (Micah 6:8)*

- Justice is that which is right for all people as exemplified in the character of God and expressed in the Word of God.

> *You shall not pervert the justice due to your poor in his lawsuit. (Exodus 23:6)*

You shall not pervert justice. You shall not show partiality, and you shall not accept a bribe, for a bribe blinds the eyes of the wise and subverts the cause of the righteous. (Deuteronomy 16:19)

Thus says the LORD: Do justice and righteousness, and deliver from the hand of the oppressor him who has been robbed. And do no wrong or violence to the resident alien, the fatherless, and the widow, nor shed innocent blood in this place. (Jeremiah 22:3)

May he judge your people with righteousness, and your poor with justice! Let the mountains bear prosperity for the people, and the hills, in righteousness! May he defend the cause of the poor of the people, give deliverance to the children of the needy, and crush the oppressor! (Psalm 72:2–4)

Give justice to the weak and the fatherless; maintain the right of the afflicted and the destitute. (Psalm 82:3)

The LORD works righteousness and justice for all who are oppressed. (Psalm 103:6)

I know that the LORD will maintain the cause of the afflicted, and will execute justice for the needy. (Psalm 140:12)

. . . who executes justice for the oppressed, who gives food to the hungry. (Psalm 146:7)

- As a result of sin, __injustice__ abounds in humanity.

Moreover, I saw under the sun that in the place of justice, even there was wickedness, and in the place of righteousness, even there was wickedness. I said in my heart, God will judge the righteous and the wicked, for there is a time for every matter and for every work. (Ecclesiastes 3:16–17)

Again I saw all the oppressions that are done under the sun. And behold, the tears of the oppressed, and they had no one to comfort them! On the side of their oppressors there was power, and there was no one to comfort them. And I thought the dead who are already dead more fortunate than the living who are still alive. But better than both is he who has not yet been and has not seen the evil deeds that are done under the sun. (Ecclesiastes 4:1–3)

- God holds his people __accountable__ for injustice.

Thus says the LORD: Do justice and righteousness, and deliver from the hand of the oppressor him who has been robbed. And do no wrong or violence to the resident alien, the fatherless, and the widow, nor shed innocent blood in this place. For if you will indeed obey this word, then there shall enter the gates of this house kings who sit on the throne of David, riding in chariots and on horses, they and their servants and their people. But if you will not obey these words, I swear by myself, declares the LORD, that this house shall become a desolation. (Jeremiah 22:3–5)

Woe to you, scribes and Pharisees, hypocrites! For you tithe mint and dill and cumin, and have neglected the weightier matters of the law: justice and mercy and faithfulness. These you ought to have done, without neglecting the others. (Matthew 23:23)

- The gospel of Jesus Christ is our __only__ hope for ultimate justice.

. . . if indeed you continue in the faith, stable and steadfast, not shifting from the hope of the gospel that you heard, which has been proclaimed in all creation under heaven, and of which I, Paul, became a minister. (Colossians 1:23)

Blessed be the God and Father of our Lord Jesus Christ! According to his great mercy, he has caused us to be born again to a living hope through the resurrection of Jesus Christ from the dead . . . (1 Peter 1:3)

  ○ Jesus perfectly reveals the character of God.

> In the beginning was the Word, and the Word was with God, and the Word was God. He was in the beginning with God. All things were made through him, and without him was not any thing made that was made. In him was life, and the life was the light of men. (John 1:1–4)

○ Jesus perfectly fulfills the Word of God.

> Do not think that I have come to abolish the Law or the Prophets; I have not come to abolish them but to fulfill them. For truly, I say to you, until heaven and earth pass away, not an iota, not a dot, will pass from the Law until all is accomplished. Therefore whoever relaxes one of the least of these commandments and teaches others to do the same will be called least in the kingdom of heaven, but whoever does them and teaches them will be called great in the kingdom of heaven. For I tell you, unless your righteousness exceeds that of the scribes and Pharisees, you will never enter the kingdom of heaven. (Matthew 5:17–20)

○ Jesus perfectly demonstrates the justice of God.

> For to us a child is born, to us a son is given; and the government shall be upon his shoulder, and his name shall be called Wonderful Counselor, Mighty God, Everlasting Father, Prince of Peace. Of the increase of his government and of peace there will be no end, on the throne of David and over his kingdom, to establish it and to uphold it with justice and with righteousness from this time forth and forevermore. The zeal of the LORD of hosts will do this. (Isaiah 9:6–8)

> I can do nothing on my own. As I hear, I judge, and my judgment is just, because I seek not my own will but the will of him who sent me. (John 5:30)

○ Jesus came to . . .
  ▪ Proclaim justice to people in all nations.

> Jesus, aware of this, withdrew from there. And many followed him, and he healed them all and ordered them not to make

him known. This was to fulfill what was spoken by the prophet Isaiah: "Behold, my servant whom I have chosen, my beloved with whom my soul is well pleased. I will put my Spirit upon him, and he will proclaim justice to the Gentiles. He will not quarrel or cry aloud, nor will anyone hear his voice in the streets; a bruised reed he will not break, and a smoldering wick he will not quench, until he brings justice to victory; and in his name the Gentiles will hope." (Matthew 12:15–21)

- Endure the judgment that people from all nations deserve.

  All we like sheep have gone astray; we have turned—every one—to his own way; and the LORD has laid on him the iniquity of us all. He was oppressed, and he was afflicted, yet he opened not his mouth; like a lamb that is led to the slaughter, and like a sheep that before its shearers is silent, so he opened not his mouth. By oppression and judgment he was taken away; and as for his generation, who considered that he was cut off out of the land of the living, stricken for the transgression of my people? And they made his grave with the wicked and with a rich man in his death, although he had done no violence, and there was no deceit in his mouth. (Isaiah 53:6–9)

  My little children, I am writing these things to you so that you may not sin. But if anyone does sin, we have an advocate with the Father, Jesus Christ the righteous. He is the propitiation for our sins, and not for ours only but also for the sins of the whole world. (1 John 2:1–2)

- Die on the cross for sinners so that anyone from any nation may be justified before God by grace through faith in him.

  But now the righteousness of God has been manifested apart from the law, although the Law and the Prophets bear witness to it—the righteousness of God through faith in Jesus Christ for all who believe. For there is no distinction: for all have sinned and fall short of the glory of God, and are

> *justified by his grace as a gift, through the redemption that is in Christ Jesus, whom God put forward as a propitiation by his blood, to be received by faith. This was to show God's righteousness, because in his divine forbearance he had passed over former sins. It was to show his righteousness at the present time, so that he might be just and the justifier of the one who has faith in Jesus.* (Romans 3:21–26)

○ Justification by faith before God leads to __works__ by faith that glorify God, including efforts to do justice.

> *What good is it, my brothers, if someone says he has faith but does not have works? Can that faith save him? If a brother or sister is poorly clothed and lacking in daily food, and one of you says to them, "Go in peace, be warmed and filled," without giving them the things needed for the body, what good is that? So also faith by itself, if it does not have works, is dead. But someone will say, "You have faith and I have works." Show me your faith apart from your works, and I will show you my faith by my works. You believe that God is one; you do well. Even the demons believe—and shudder! Do you want to be shown, you foolish person, that faith apart from works is useless? Was not Abraham our father justified by works when he offered up his son Isaac on the altar? You see that faith was active along with his works, and faith was completed by his works; and the Scripture was fulfilled that says, "Abraham believed God, and it was counted to him as righteousness"—and he was called a friend of God. You see that a person is justified by works and not by faith alone. And in the same way was not also Rahab the prostitute justified by works when she received the messengers and sent them out by another way? For as the body apart from the spirit is dead, so also faith apart from works is dead.* (James 2:14–26)

- Loving God with all our hearts.
- Loving others as ourselves.

> *And he said to him, "You shall love the Lord your God with all your heart and with all your soul and with all your mind.*

> *This is the great and first commandment. And a second is like it: You shall love your neighbor as yourself. On these two commandments depend all the Law and the Prophets."* (Matthew 22:37–40)

- We do justice by _proclaiming_ the gospel among all people.

> *But you will receive power when the Holy Spirit has come upon you, and you will be my witnesses in Jerusalem and in all Judea and Samaria, and to the end of the earth.* (Acts 1:8)

> *For I will not venture to speak of anything except what Christ has accomplished through me to bring the Gentiles to obedience— by word and deed, by the power of signs and wonders, by the power of the Spirit of God—so that from Jerusalem and all the way around to Illyricum I have fulfilled the ministry of the gospel of Christ; and thus I make it my ambition to preach the gospel, not where Christ has already been named, lest I build on someone else's foundation, but as it is written, "Those who have never been told of him will see, and those who have never heard will understand."* (Romans 15:18-21)

- We do justice by doing and teaching others to _____ everything Christ has commanded us.

> *Go therefore and make disciples of all nations, baptizing them in the name of the Father and of the Son and of the Holy Spirit . . .* (Matthew 28:19)

- o We model and teach justice and mercy in our families.

> *And now, O Israel, listen to the statutes and the rules that I am teaching you, and do them, that you may live, and go in and take possession of the land that the LORD, the God of your fathers, is giving you. You shall not add to the word that I command you, nor take from it, that you may keep the commandments of the LORD your God that I command you. Your*

eyes have seen what the LORD did at Baal-peor, for the LORD your God destroyed from among you all the men who followed the Baal of Peor. But you who held fast to the LORD your God are all alive today. See, I have taught you statutes and rules, as the LORD my God commanded me, that you should do them in the land that you are entering to take possession of it. Keep them and do them, for that will be your wisdom and your understanding in the sight of the peoples, who, when they hear all these statutes, will say, "Surely this great nation is a wise and understanding people." For what great nation is there that has a god so near to it as the LORD our God is to us, whenever we call upon him? And what great nation is there, that has statutes and rules so righteous as all this law that I set before you today? Only take care, and keep your soul diligently, lest you forget the things that your eyes have seen, and lest they depart from your heart all the days of your life. Make them known to your children and your children's children . . . (Deuteronomy 4:1–9)

○ We work hard and honestly at our jobs that contribute to the good of society and enable us to share our resources with others.

Now we command you, brothers, in the name of our Lord Jesus Christ, that you keep away from any brother who is walking in idleness and not in accord with the tradition that you received from us. For you yourselves know how you ought to imitate us, because we were not idle when we were with you, nor did we eat anyone's bread without paying for it, but with toil and labor we worked night and day, that we might not be a burden to any of you. It was not because we do not have that right, but to give you in ourselves an example to imitate. For even when we were with you, we would give you this command: If anyone is not willing to work, let him not eat. For we hear that some among you walk in idleness, not busy at work, but busybodies. Now such persons we command and encourage in the Lord Jesus Christ to do their work quietly and to earn their own living. As for you, brothers, do not grow weary in doing good. If anyone does not obey what we say in this letter, take note of that person, and have nothing to do with him, that he may be ashamed. Do not regard him as an enemy, but warn him as a brother. (2 Thessalonians 3:6–15)

Let the thief no longer steal, but rather let him labor, doing honest work with his own hands, so that he may have something to share with anyone in need. (Ephesians 4:28)

○ We give generously and sacrificially of our resources to people in need.

As for the rich in this present age, charge them not to be haughty, nor to set their hopes on the uncertainty of riches, but on God, who richly provides us with everything to enjoy. They are to do good, to be rich in good works, to be generous and ready to share, thus storing up treasure for themselves as a good foundation for the future, so that they may take hold of that which is truly life. (1 Timothy 6:17–19)

○ We steward advantages we have for the sake of the disadvantaged.

We want you to know, brothers, about the grace of God that has been given among the churches of Macedonia, for in a severe test of affliction, their abundance of joy and their extreme poverty have overflowed in a wealth of generosity on their part. For they gave according to their means, as I can testify, and beyond their means, of their own accord, begging us earnestly for the favor of taking part in the relief of the saints—and this, not as we expected, but they gave themselves first to the Lord and then by the will of God to us. Accordingly, we urged Titus that as he had started, so he should complete among you this act of grace. But as you excel in everything—in faith, in speech, in knowledge, in all earnestness, and in our love for you—see that you excel in this act of grace also. I say this not as a command, but to prove by the earnestness of others that your love also is genuine. For you know the grace of our Lord Jesus Christ, that though he was rich, yet for your sake he became poor, so that you by his poverty might become rich. (2 Corinthians 8:1–9)

○ We use any leadership, authority, or influence we have to
_____ others.

> And Jesus called them to him and said to them, "You know that
> those who are considered rulers of the Gentiles lord it over them,
> and their great ones exercise authority over them. But it shall
> not be so among you. But whoever would be great among you
> must be your servant, and whoever would be first among you
> must be slave of all. For even the Son of Man came not to be
> served but to serve, and to give his life as a ransom for many."
> (Mark 10:42–45)

○ We care for widows, orphans, and sojourners.

> Religion that is pure and undefiled before God the Father is this:
> to visit orphans and widows in their affliction, and to keep oneself
> unstained from the world. (James 1:17)

> You shall treat the stranger who sojourns with you as the native
> among you, and you shall love him as yourself, for you were
> strangers in the land of Egypt: I am the LORD your God.
> (Leviticus 19:34)

○ We understand the needs and defend the rights of the poor.

> A righteous man knows the rights of the poor; a wicked man
> does not understand such knowledge. (Proverbs 29:7)

> Open your mouth for the mute, for the rights of all who are
> destitute. Open your mouth, judge righteously, defend the rights
> of the poor and needy. (Proverbs 31:8–9)

○ We correct _____.

> . . . learn to do good; seek justice, correct oppression; bring
> justice to the fatherless, plead the widow's cause. (Isaiah 1:17)

○ We refuse to show partiality.

My brothers, show no partiality as you hold the faith in our Lord Jesus Christ, the Lord of glory. For if a man wearing a gold ring and fine clothing comes into your assembly, and a poor man in shabby clothing also comes in, and if you pay attention to the one who wears the fine clothing and say, "You sit here in a good place," while you say to the poor man, "You stand over there," or, "Sit down at my feet," have you not then made distinctions among yourselves and become judges with evil thoughts? Listen, my beloved brothers, has not God chosen those who are poor in the world to be rich in faith and heirs of the kingdom, which he has promised to those who love him? But you have dishonored the poor man. Are not the rich the ones who oppress you, and the ones who drag you into court? Are they not the ones who blaspheme the honorable name by which you were called? (James 2:1–7)

○ We honor, pray for, and subject ourselves to government leaders under God.

Let every person be subject to the governing authorities. For there is no authority except from God, and those that exist have been instituted by God. Therefore whoever resists the authorities resists what God has appointed, and those who resist will incur judgment. For rulers are not a terror to good conduct, but to bad. Would you have no fear of the one who is in authority? Then do what is good, and you will receive his approval, for he is God's servant for your good. But if you do wrong, be afraid, for he does not bear the sword in vain. For he is the servant of God, an avenger who carries out God's wrath on the wrongdoer. Therefore one must be in subjection, not only to avoid God's wrath but also for the sake of conscience. (Romans 13:1–5)

Be subject for the Lord's sake to every human institution, whether it be to the emperor as supreme, or to governors as sent by him to punish those who do evil and to praise those who do good. For this is the will of God, that by doing good you should put to silence the ignorance of foolish people. Live as people who are free, not using your freedom as a cover-up for evil, but living as

*servants of God. Honor everyone. Love the brotherhood. Fear
God. Honor the emperor.* (1 Peter 2:13–17)

○ We live to _____ righteousness at all times.

*Blessed are they who observe justice, who do righteousness at all
times!* (Psalm 106:3)

- To the extent that we are able and have opportunity according
to God's leadership in our lives, we _____ justice
in the world around us.

*Therefore be imitators of God, as beloved children. And walk in
love, as Christ loved us and gave himself up for us, a fragrant
offering and sacrifice to God.* (Ephesians 5:1–2)

*Give the king your justice, O God, and your righteousness to
the royal son! May he judge your people with righteousness, and
your poor with justice! Let the mountains bear prosperity for the
people, and the hills, in righteousness! May he defend the cause
of the poor of the people, give deliverance to the children of the
needy, and crush the oppressor! May they fear you while the sun
endures, and as long as the moon, throughout all generations!
May he be like rain that falls on the mown grass, like showers
that water the earth! In his days may the righteous flourish, and
peace abound, till the moon be no more! May he have dominion
from sea to sea, and from the River to the ends of the earth!
May desert tribes bow down before him, and his enemies lick the
dust! May the kings of Tarshish and of the coastlands render him
tribute; may the kings of Sheba and Seba bring gifts! May all
kings fall down before him, all nations serve him! For he delivers
the needy when he calls, the poor and him who has no helper.
He has pity on the weak and the needy, and saves the lives of the
needy. From oppression and violence he redeems their life, and
precious is their blood in his sight. Long may he live; may gold of
Sheba be given to him! May prayer be made for him continually,
and blessings invoked for him all the day! May there be abundance of grain in the land; on the tops of the mountains may it*

wave; may its fruit be like Lebanon; and may people blossom in the cities like the grass of the field! May his name endure forever, his fame continue as long as the sun! May people be blessed in him, all nations call him blessed! Blessed be the LORD, the God of Israel, who alone does wondrous things. Blessed be his glorious name forever; may the whole earth be filled with his glory! Amen and Amen! The prayers of David, the son of Jesse, are ended. (Psalm 72:1–20)

• We long for the day when Jesus the Judge returns and his justice _____ on the earth.

How long, O LORD? Will you forget me forever? How long will you hide your face from me? How long must I take counsel in my soul and have sorrow in my heart all the day? How long shall my enemy be exalted over me? (Psalm 13:1–2)

Pray then like this: "Our Father in heaven, hallowed be your name. Your kingdom come, your will be done, on earth as it is in heaven." (Matthew 6:9–10)

When he opened the fifth seal, I saw under the altar the souls of those who had been slain for the word of God and for the witness they had borne. They cried out with a loud voice, "O Sovereign Lord, holy and true, how long before you will judge and avenge our blood on those who dwell on the earth?" Then they were each given a white robe and told to rest a little longer, until the number of their fellow servants and their brothers should be complete, who were to be killed as they themselves had been. (Revelation 6:9–11)

• As long as sin remains, this world will not be perfectly just.

• We pray for injustice to end.

• We pray for God's kingdom to come.

• We live to hasten his coming.

Since all these things are thus to be dissolved, what sort of people ought you to be in lives of holiness and godliness, waiting for and hastening the coming of the day of God, because of which the heavens will be set on fire and dissolved, and the heavenly bodies will melt as they burn! But according to his promise we are waiting for new heavens and a new earth in which righteousness dwells. (2 Peter 3:11–13)

He who testifies to these things says, "Surely I am coming soon." Amen. Come, Lord Jesus! (Revelation 22:20)

CONTEMPORARY
APPLICATIONS

Please God with
your body
not
please your body

HUMANITY AND SEXUALITY

Your body was created by God for his _____ and for your earthly and eternal _____.

"All things are lawful for me," but not all things are helpful. "All things are lawful for me," but I will not be dominated by anything. "Food is meant for the stomach and the stomach for food"—and God will destroy both one and the other. The body is not meant for sexual immorality, but for the Lord, and the Lord for the body. And God raised the Lord and will also raise us up by his power. Do you not know that your bodies are members of Christ? Shall I then take the members of Christ and make them members of a prostitute? Never! Or do you not know that he who is joined to a prostitute becomes one body with her? For, as it is written, "The two will become one flesh." But he who is joined to the Lord becomes one spirit with him. Flee from sexual immorality. Every other sin a person commits is outside the body, but the sexually immoral person sins against his own body. (1 Corinthians 6:12–18)

Behold! I tell you a mystery. We shall not all sleep, but we shall all be changed, in a moment, in the twinkling of an eye, at the last trumpet. For the trumpet will sound, and the dead will be raised imperishable, and we shall be changed. For this perishable body must put on the imperishable, and this mortal body must put on immortality. When the perishable puts on the imperishable, and the mortal puts on immortality, then shall come to pass the saying that is written: "Death is swallowed up in victory." "O death, where is your victory? O death, where is your sting?" The sting of death is sin, and the power of sin is the law. But thanks be to God, who gives us the victory through our Lord Jesus Christ. (1 Corinthians 15:51–57)

In this broken world, we all have broken _____.

- Bodily sin harms inevitably.
- Bodily sin controls quickly.
- Bodily sin devastates painfully.
- Bodily sin condemns eternally.

Or do you not know that the unrighteous will not inherit the kingdom of God? Do not be deceived: neither the sexually immoral, nor idolaters, nor adulterers, nor men who practice homosexuality, nor thieves, nor the greedy, nor drunkards, nor revilers, nor swindlers will inherit the kingdom of God.
(1 Corinthians 6:9–10)

Jesus gave his body to make your body __new__ .

And such were some of you. But you were washed, you were sanctified, you were justified in the name of the Lord Jesus Christ and by the Spirit of our God. (1 Corinthians 6:11)

Or do you not know that your body is a temple of the Holy Spirit within you, whom you have from God? You are not your own, for you were bought with a price. So glorify God in your body.
(1 Corinthians 6:19–20)

As men and women made in God's image, God commands us to __flee__ **sexual immorality.**

Flee from sexual immorality. Every other sin a person commits is outside the body, but the sexually immoral person sins against his own body. (1 Corinthians 6:18)

Finally, then, brothers, we ask and urge you in the Lord Jesus, that as you received from us how you ought to walk and to please God, just as you are doing, that you do so more and more. For you know what instructions we gave you through the Lord Jesus. For this is the will of God, your sanctification: that you abstain from sexual immorality; that each one of you know how to control his own body in holiness and honor, not in the passion of lust like the Gentiles who do not know God; that no one transgress and wrong his brother in this matter, because the Lord is an avenger in all these things, as we told you beforehand and solemnly warned you. For God has not called us for impurity, but in holiness. Therefore whoever disregards

this, disregards not man but God, who gives his Holy Spirit to you.
(1 Thessalonians 4:1–8)

- Whenever God gives us a negative command . . .
  - God is pointing to something _____.
  - God is protecting us from something _____.

- Flee sexual immorality = Flee any and all sexual activity outside of marriage between a husband and a wife.
  - There is not one place in God's Word where God celebrates sexual activity outside of marriage between a husband and a wife.
  - None of us is _____ to sexual temptation.
  - All of us are _____ with a bent toward sexual sin.
  - Sexual immorality in a broken world . . .
    - Sexual desire: We want . . .
    - Sexual identity: We are . . .
    - Sexual activity: We act . . .

  > *There is a way that seems right to a man, but its end is the way to death.* (Proverbs 14:12)

As men and women made in God's image, God calls us to _Satisfaction_ **in him and his Word.**

> *Jesus said to them, "I am the bread of life; whoever comes to me shall not hunger, and whoever believes in me shall never thirst."* (John 6:35)

> *And he said to all, "If anyone would come after me, let him deny himself and take up his cross daily and follow me. For whoever would save his life will lose it, but whoever loses his life for my sake will save it."* (Luke 9:23–24)

- The call to follow Jesus is ultimately not a call to unfulfilled desire.
- The call to follow Jesus is ultimately a call to _____ of our deepest desires in dying to ourselves and living in Jesus.

I have been crucified with Christ. It is no longer I who live, but Christ who lives in me. And the life I now live in the flesh I live by faith in the Son of God, who loved me and gave himself for me. (Galatians 2:20)

FOR REFLECTION

How are you tempted to go outside of God's good design for your body in your thoughts, desires, and actions?

HUMANITY AND RACE

Regardless of who we are or what we look like, we share _equal_ dignity and value before God and one another.

> The man called his wife's name Eve, because she was the mother of all living. (Genesis 3:20)

- We all have a common ancestry.
- We are equal members of a common _____.

We are united in our humanity, yet diverse in our _____.

> These are the generations of the sons of Noah, Shem, Ham, and Japheth. Sons were born to them after the flood. (Genesis 10:1)

> Therefore its name was called Babel, because there the LORD confused the language of all the earth. And from there the LORD dispersed them over the face of all the earth. (Genesis 11:9)

- Various clans.
- Distant lands.
- Separate nations.
- Assorted languages.
- Extensive and extraordinary diversity with basic and beautiful unity.

> The God who made the world and everything in it, being Lord of heaven and earth, does not live in temples made by man, nor is he served by human hands, as though he needed anything, since he himself gives to all mankind life and breath and everything. And he made from one man every nation of mankind to live on all the face of the earth, having determined allotted periods and the boundaries of their dwelling place, that they should seek God, and perhaps feel their way toward him and find him. Yet he is actually not far from each one of us, for "In him we live and move and have our being"; as even some of your own poets have said, "For we are indeed his offspring." Being then God's

offspring, we ought not to think that the divine being is like gold or silver or stone, an image formed by the art and imagination of man. (Acts 17:24–29)

God loves and pursues all people in __all__ people groups.

For God so loved the world, that he gave his only Son, that whoever believes in him should not perish but have eternal life. (John 3:16)

He is the propitiation for our sins, and not for ours only but also for the sins of the whole world. (1 John 2:2)

The Lord is not slow to fulfill his promise as some count slowness, but is patient toward you, not wishing that any should perish, but that all should reach repentance. (2 Peter 3:9)

Now the LORD said to Abram, "Go from your country and your kindred and your father's house to the land that I will show you. And I will make of you a great nation, and I will bless you and make your name great, so that you will be a blessing. I will bless those who bless you, and him who dishonors you I will curse, and in you all the families of the earth shall be blessed." (Genesis 12:1–3)

May God be gracious to us and bless us and make his face to shine upon us, Selah that your way may be known on earth, your saving power among all nations. Let the peoples praise you, O God; let all the peoples praise you! Let the nations be glad and sing for joy, for you judge the peoples with equity and guide the nations upon earth. Selah Let the peoples praise you, O God; let all the peoples praise you! The earth has yielded its increase; God, our God, shall bless us. God shall bless us; let all the ends of the earth fear him! (Psalm 67:1–7)

And Jesus came and said to them, "All authority in heaven and on earth has been given to me. Go therefore and make disciples of all nations, baptizing them in the name of the Father and of the Son and of the Holy Spirit, teaching them to observe all that I have commanded

you. And behold, I am with you always, to the end of the age."
(Matthew 28:18–20)

But you will receive power when the Holy Spirit has come upon you, and you will be my witnesses in Jerusalem and in all Judea and Samaria, and to the end of the earth. (Acts 1:8)

And after there had been much debate, Peter stood up and said to them, "Brothers, you know that in the early days God made a choice among you, that by my mouth the Gentiles should hear the word of the gospel and believe. And God, who knows the heart, bore witness to them, by giving them the Holy Spirit just as he did to us, and he made no distinction between us and them, having cleansed their hearts by faith." (Acts 15:7–9)

Therefore let it be known to you that this salvation of God has been sent to the Gentiles; they will listen. (Acts 28:28)

- Repentance and forgiveness of sins must be proclaimed in all people groups.

  Then he opened their minds to understand the Scriptures, and said to them, "Thus it is written, that the Christ should suffer and on the third day rise from the dead, and that repentance for the forgiveness of sins should be proclaimed in his name to all nations, beginning from Jerusalem. You are witnesses of these things. And behold, I am sending the promise of my Father upon you. But stay in the city until you are clothed with power from on high." (Luke 24:45–49)

- God is worthy of glory, honor, and praise from all people groups.

  And they sang a new song, saying, "Worthy are you to take the scroll and to open its seals, for you were slain, and by your blood you ransomed people for God from every tribe and language and people and nation, and you have made them a kingdom and priests to our God, and they shall reign on the earth." (Revelation 5:9–10)

After this I looked, and behold, a great multitude that no one could number, from every nation, from all tribes and peoples and languages, standing before the throne and before the Lamb, clothed in white robes, with palm branches in their hands, and crying out with a loud voice, "Salvation belongs to our God who sits on the throne, and to the Lamb!" (Revelation 7:9–10)

The church is a _chosen_ race, a holy nation, and a distinct people for God's own possession.

But you are a chosen race, a royal priesthood, a holy nation, a people for his own possession, that you may proclaim the excellencies of him who called you out of darkness into his marvelous light. Once you were not a people, but now you are God's people; once you had not received mercy, but now you have received mercy. (1 Peter 2:9–10)

- One physical race.
- Two _spiritual_ races.

Therefore, just as sin came into the world through one man, and death through sin, and so death spread to all men because all sinned—for sin indeed was in the world before the law was given, but sin is not counted where there is no law. Yet death reigned from Adam to Moses, even over those whose sinning was not like the transgression of Adam, who was a type of the one who was to come. But the free gift is not like the trespass. For if many died through one man's trespass, much more have the grace of God and the free gift by the grace of that one man Jesus Christ abounded for many. And the free gift is not like the result of that one man's sin. For the judgment following one trespass brought condemnation, but the free gift following many trespasses brought justification. For if, because of one man's trespass, death reigned through that one man, much more will those who receive the abundance of grace and the free gift of righteousness reign in life through the one man Jesus Christ. Therefore, as one trespass led to condemnation for all men, so one act of righteousness leads to justification and life for all men. For as by the one man's disobedience the many were made sinners, so by the one man's obedience the many will be made righteous. Now the law came in to increase the trespass, but where sin increased, grace abounded all the more, so that, as sin reigned in death, grace also might reign through righteousness leading to eternal life through Jesus Christ our Lord. (Romans 5:12–21)

  - ○ In Adam: Condemned by God because of sin.
  - ○ In Christ: Redeemed by God through faith in Jesus.

- Humanity's standing before God cannot be improved by . . .
  - ○ Individual accomplishment.

    We have all become like one who is unclean, and all our righteous deeds are like a polluted garment. We all fade like a leaf, and our iniquities, like the wind, take us away. (Isaiah 64:6)

  - ○ Biological bloodline.

    But to all who did receive him, who believed in his name, he gave the right to become children of God, who were born, not of blood nor of the will of the flesh nor of the will of man, but of God. (John 1:12–13)

- Justification before God is only possible . . .

    For by grace you have been saved through faith. And this is not your own doing; it is the gift of God, not a result of works, so that no one may boast. (Ephesians 2:8–9)

  - ○ By grace alone.
  - ○ Through faith alone.
  - ○ In Jesus alone.

- Jesus' revolutionary bloodline creates a counter-cultural family of multi-ethnic unity called the __church__.

    Pay careful attention to yourselves and to all the flock, in which the Holy Spirit has made you overseers, to care for the church of God, which he obtained with his own blood. (Acts 20:28)

○ Dividing walls of hostility are destroyed.

> *Therefore remember that at one time you Gentiles in the flesh, called "the uncircumcision" by what is called the circumcision, which is made in the flesh by hands—remember that you were at that time separated from Christ, alienated from the commonwealth of Israel and strangers to the covenants of promise, having no hope and without God in the world. But now in Christ Jesus you who once were far off have been brought near by the blood of Christ. For he himself is our peace, who has made us both one and has broken down in his flesh the dividing wall of hostility by abolishing the law of commandments expressed in ordinances, that he might create in himself one new man in place of the two, so making peace, and might reconcile us both to God in one body through the cross, thereby killing the hostility. And he came and preached peace to you who were far off and peace to those who were near. For through him we both have access in one Spirit to the Father. So then you are no longer strangers and aliens, but you are fellow citizens with the saints and members of the household of God, built on the foundation of the apostles and prophets, Christ Jesus himself being the cornerstone, in whom the whole structure, being joined together, grows into a holy temple in the Lord. In him you also are being built together into a dwelling place for God by the Spirit. (Ephesians 2:11–22)*

> "While homogeneity in churches simply reinforces the status quo of society, the biblical evidence shows us that the gospel broke down and cut across ethnic, social, economic, and cultural barriers in ways never before seen in history." – Aubrey Sequeira[26]

○ Reconciliation before God has paved the way for
  reconciliation with each other.

> *And you, who once were alienated and hostile in mind, doing evil deeds, he has now reconciled in his body of flesh by his death, in order to present you holy and blameless and above reproach before him, if indeed you continue in the faith, stable and steadfast, not shifting from the hope of the gospel that you*

heard, which has been proclaimed in all creation under heaven, and of which I, Paul, became a minister. (Colossians 1:21–23)

Put to death therefore what is earthly in you: sexual immorality, impurity, passion, evil desire, and covetousness, which is idolatry. On account of these the wrath of God is coming. In these you too once walked, when you were living in them. But now you must put them all away: anger, wrath, malice, slander, and obscene talk from your mouth. Do not lie to one another, seeing that you have put off the old self with its practices and have put on the new self, which is being renewed in knowledge after the image of its creator. Here there is not Greek and Jew, circumcised and uncircumcised, barbarian, Scythian, slave, free; but Christ is all, and in all. (Colossians 3:5–11)

○ We are one eternal family.

I hope to come to you soon, but I am writing these things to you so that, if I delay, you may know how one ought to behave in the household of God, which is the church of the living God, a pillar and buttress of the truth. (1 Timothy 3:14–15)

○ We share one Holy Spirit.

For in one Spirit we were all baptized into one body—Jews or Greeks, slaves or free—and all were made to drink of one Spirit. (1 Corinthians 12:13)

○ We have one Heavenly __Father__.

. . . one Lord, one faith, one baptism, one God and Father of all, who is over all and through all and in all. (Ephesians 4:5–6)

___Racism___ is a fundamental perversion of God's good design for humanity.

- As sinners, we pervert a biblical concept of race by classifying groups of people into different "races" based on arbitrary characteristics in order to assign different values and distinct advantages to some groups over others.
    - Skin tone
    - Hair texture
    - Facial features
    - Class
    - Caste
    - Geography
    - Ancestry
    - Language

- In the process of denying our shared roots in the human race by devising a hierarchy of different "races," we commit the _____ of racism:
    - Valuing one "race" over another in our thoughts, feelings, words, and actions, or . . .
    - Devaluing one "race" beneath another in our thoughts, feelings, words, and actions.
    - Expressions of racism . . .
        - Thoughts
        - Feelings
        - Words
        - Actions
        - Expectations
        - Relationships
        - Laws
        - Policies
        - Procedures
        - Systems and structures (comprising much of the above)

    - Expressions of racism are rooted in . . .
        - Pride before God.

> Now the serpent was more crafty than any other beast of the field that the LORD God had made. He said to the woman, "Did God actually say, 'You shall not eat of any tree in the

garden'?" And the woman said to the serpent, "We may eat of the fruit of the trees in the garden, but God said, 'You shall not eat of the fruit of the tree that is in the midst of the garden, neither shall you touch it, lest you die.'" But the serpent said to the woman, "You will not surely die. For God knows that when you eat of it your eyes will be opened, and you will be like God, knowing good and evil." So when the woman saw that the tree was good for food, and that it was a delight to the eyes, and that the tree was to be desired to make one wise, she took of its fruit and ate, and she also gave some to her husband who was with her, and he ate. Then the eyes of both were opened, and they knew that they were naked. And they sewed fig leaves together and made themselves loincloths. (Genesis 3:1–7)

- Pride before others.

But it displeased Jonah exceedingly, and he was angry. And he prayed to the Lord and said, "O Lord, is not this what I said when I was yet in my country? That is why I made haste to flee to Tarshish; for I knew that you are a gracious God and merciful, slow to anger and abounding in steadfast love, and relenting from disaster. Therefore now, O Lord, please take my life from me, for it is better for me to die than to live." And the Lord said, "Do you do well to be angry?" Jonah went out of the city and sat to the east of the city and made a booth for himself there. He sat under it in the shade, till he should see what would become of the city. Now the Lord God appointed a plant and made it come up over Jonah, that it might be a shade over his head, to save him from his discomfort. So Jonah was exceedingly glad because of the plant. But when dawn came up the next day, God appointed a worm that attacked the plant, so that it withered. When the sun rose, God appointed a scorching east wind, and the sun beat down on the head of Jonah so that he was faint. And he asked that he might die and said, "It is better for me to die than to live." But God said to Jonah, "Do you do well to be angry for the plant?" And he said, "Yes, I do well to be angry, angry enough to die." And the Lord said, "You pity the plant, for which you did not labor, nor did you make it grow, which came into being in a night and perished in a night. And should not I pity Nineveh, that great city, in which there are more than 120,000 persons who do not know their right hand from their left, and also much cattle?" (Jonah 4:1–11)

- Partiality toward people.

  And behold, a lawyer stood up to put him to the test, saying, "Teacher, what shall I do to inherit eternal life?" He said to him, "What is written in the Law? How do you read it?" And he answered, "You shall love the Lord your God with all your heart and with all your soul and with all your strength and with all your mind, and your neighbor as yourself." And he said to him, "You have answered correctly; do this, and you will live." But he, desiring to justify himself, said to Jesus, "And who is my neighbor?" Jesus replied, "A man was going down from Jerusalem to Jericho, and he fell among robbers, who stripped him and beat him and departed, leaving him half dead. Now by chance a priest was going down that road, and when he saw him he passed by on the other side. So likewise a Levite, when he came to the place and saw him, passed by on the other side. But a Samaritan, as he journeyed, came to where he was, and when he saw him, he had compassion. He went to him and bound up his wounds, pouring on oil and wine. Then he set him on his own animal and brought him to an inn and took care of him. And the next day he took out two denarii and gave them to the innkeeper, saying, 'Take care of him, and whatever more you spend, I will repay you when I come back.' Which of these three, do you think, proved to be a neighbor to the man who fell among the robbers?" He said, "The one who showed him mercy." And Jesus said to him, "You go, and do likewise." (Luke 10:25–37)

- Propensity toward prejudice.

> *So Peter opened his mouth and said: "Truly I understand that God shows no partiality . . ."* (Acts 10:34)

- Personal preferences.

God calls us to _____ racism in every way.

> *So Peter opened his mouth and said: "Truly I understand that God shows no partiality, but in every nation anyone who fears him and does what is right is acceptable to him. As for the word that he sent to Israel, preaching good news of peace through Jesus Christ (he is Lord of all), you yourselves know what happened throughout all Judea, beginning from Galilee after the baptism that John proclaimed: how God anointed Jesus of Nazareth with the Holy Spirit and with power. He went about doing good and healing all who were oppressed by the devil, for God was with him. And we are witnesses of all that he did both in the country of the Jews and in Jerusalem. They put him to death by hanging him on a tree, but God raised him on the third day and made him to appear, not to all the people but to us who had been chosen by God as witnesses, who ate and drank with him after he rose from the dead. And he commanded us to preach to the people and to testify that he is the one appointed by God to be judge of the living and the dead. To him all the prophets bear witness that everyone who believes in him receives forgiveness of sins through his name."* (Acts 10:34–43)

- We reject any and all semblance of a hierarchy of different "races."

- We repel any and every inclination in us to exalt or devalue any "race" over or beneath another.

  > "Race prejudice can't be talked down, it must be lived down."
  > – Francis Grimke[27]

- We refrain from . . .
  - Partial ways of relating.

> *My brothers, show no partiality as you hold the faith in our Lord Jesus Christ, the Lord of glory.* (James 2:1)

- Biased ways of thinking.

> *Finally, brothers, whatever is true, whatever is honorable, whatever is just, whatever is pure, whatever is lovely, whatever is commendable, if there is any excellence, if there is anything worthy of praise, think about these things. What you have learned and received and heard and seen in me—practice these things, and the God of peace will be with you.* (Philippians 4:8–9)

- Derogatory ways of speaking.

> *Let no corrupting talk come out of your mouths, but only such as is good for building up, as fits the occasion, that it may give grace to those who hear. And do not grieve the Holy Spirit of God, by whom you were sealed for the day of redemption. Let all bitterness and wrath and anger and clamor and slander be put away from you, along with all malice. Be kind to one another, tenderhearted, forgiving one another, as God in Christ forgave you.* (Ephesians 4:29–32)

- Discriminatory ways of acting.

> *So whatever you wish that others would do to you, do also to them, for this is the Law and the Prophets.* (Matthew 7:12)

- We repent of all intentional expressions of racism.

> *Repent therefore, and turn back, that your sins may be blotted out . . .* (Acts 3:19)

- We recognize how our actions can unintentionally either express racism or contribute to the effects of racism.

> *Who can discern his errors? Declare me innocent from hidden faults. Keep back your servant also from presumptuous sins; let*

> them not have dominion over me! Then I shall be blameless, and
> innocent of great transgression. Let the words of my mouth and
> the meditation of my heart be acceptable in your sight, O LORD,
> my rock and my redeemer. (Psalm 19:12–14)

- We resist any way in which racism around us (from our family
  upbringing to our surrounding culture) has _____
  our thoughts, feelings, words, or actions regarding different groups
  of people.

> Do not be conformed to this world, but be transformed by the
> renewal of your mind, that by testing you may discern what is
> the will of God, what is good and acceptable and perfect.
> (Romans 12:2)

> Now therefore fear the LORD and serve him in sincerity and in
> faithfulness. Put away the gods that your fathers served beyond
> the River and in Egypt, and serve the LORD. And if it is evil in
> your eyes to serve the LORD, choose this day whom you will
> serve, whether the gods your fathers served in the region
> beyond the River, or the gods of the Amorites in whose land
> you dwell. But as for me and my house, we will serve the LORD.
> (Joshua 24:14–15)

- We rejoice in all the ways God _____ works in
  our hearts to overcome evidences or expressions of racism in and
  around us.

**God calls us to commit ourselves to _____ multi-ethnic
community.**

- We appreciate our ethnic differences without assigning more or less
  value to them.

> There is neither Jew nor Greek, there is neither slave nor free,
> there is no male and female, for you are all one in Christ Jesus.
> (Galatians 3:28)

- ○ We do not disregard these differences.
- ○ We do not discount these differences.
- ○ We do not erase these differences.

- We see our diversity as God sees our diversity: a stunning portrait of his _____ that exalts his glory as our Creator.

> After this I looked, and behold, a great multitude that no one could number, from every nation, from all tribes and peoples and languages, standing before the throne and before the Lamb, clothed in white robes, with palm branches in their hands, and crying out with a loud voice, "Salvation belongs to our God who sits on the throne, and to the Lamb!" (Revelation 7:9–10)

- We listen to, learn from, lament with, and love one another.

> Know this, my beloved brothers: let every person be quick to hear, slow to speak, slow to anger; for the anger of man does not produce the righteousness of God. Therefore put away all filthiness and rampant wickedness and receive with meekness the implanted word, which is able to save your souls. (James 1:19–21)

> A fool takes no pleasure in understanding, but only in expressing his opinion. (Proverbs 18:2)

> Rejoice with those who rejoice, weep with those who weep. (Romans 12:15)

> Love is patient and kind; love does not envy or boast; it is not arrogant or rude. It does not insist on its own way; it is not irritable or resentful; it does not rejoice at wrongdoing, but rejoices with the truth. Love bears all things, believes all things, hopes all things, endures all things. Love never ends. As for prophecies, they will pass away; as for tongues, they will cease; as for knowledge, it will pass away. (1 Corinthians 13:4–8)

- We don't assign or attribute _____ or _____ to one another for expressions of racism in others, including . . .

The soul who sins shall die. The son shall not suffer for the iniquity of the father, nor the father suffer for the iniquity of the son. The righteousness of the righteous shall be upon himself, and the wickedness of the wicked shall be upon himself. (Ezekiel 18:20)

- ○ Those who have gone before us.
- ○ Those who look like us.
- ○ Sin for which we have repented.

    There is therefore now no condemnation for those who are in Christ Jesus. (Romans 8:1)

    Therefore, confess your sins to one another and pray for one another, that you may be healed. The prayer of a righteous person has great power as it is working. (James 5:16)

- We grieve over the existence and effects of racism.

    Hot indignation seizes me because of the wicked, who forsake your law. (Psalm 119:53)

    And the LORD said to him, "Pass through the city, through Jerusalem, and put a mark on the foreheads of the men who sigh and groan over all the abominations that are committed in it." (Ezekiel 9:4)

    For godly grief produces a repentance that leads to salvation without regret, whereas worldly grief produces death. (2 Corinthians 7:10)

- We appropriately confess corporate sins of racism and take appropriate steps of repentance.

    Now, therefore, our God, the great, the mighty, and the awesome God, who keeps covenant and steadfast love, let not all the hardship seem little to you that has come upon us, upon our kings, our princes, our priests, our prophets, our fathers, and all your people, since the time of the kings of Assyria until this day.

Yet you have been righteous in all that has come upon us, for you have dealt faithfully and we have acted wickedly. Our kings, our princes, our priests, and our fathers have not kept your law or paid attention to your commandments and your warnings that you gave them. Even in their own kingdom, and amid your great goodness that you gave them, and in the large and rich land that you set before them, they did not serve you or turn from their wicked works. Behold, we are slaves this day; in the land that you gave to our fathers to enjoy its fruit and its good gifts, behold, we are slaves. And its rich yield goes to the kings whom you have set over us because of our sins. They rule over our bodies and over our livestock as they please, and we are in great distress. (Nehemiah 9:32–37)

Both we and our fathers have sinned; we have committed iniquity; we have done wickedness. (Psalm 106:6)

And I said: "Woe is me! For I am lost; for I am a man of unclean lips, and I dwell in the midst of a people of unclean lips; for my eyes have seen the King, the LORD of hosts!" (Isaiah 6:5)

- We are zealous in the present not to prolong or replicate in any way racial injustice from the _____.

But the high places were not removed; the people still sacrificed and made offerings on the high places. (2 Kings 14:4)

- We _____ our hearts humbly and continually for expressions of racism with the help of . . .

Search me, O God, and know my heart! Try me and know my thoughts! And see if there be any grievous way in me, and lead me in the way everlasting! (Psalm 139:23–24)

Examine yourselves, to see whether you are in the faith. Test yourselves. Or do you not realize this about yourselves, that Jesus Christ is in you?—unless indeed you fail to meet the test! (2 Corinthians 13:5)

- The Holy Spirit.
- Brothers and sisters in Christ.
  - They enable us to see sin in us and sin's effects around us in ways we might not see ourselves.

> *If your brother sins against you, go and tell him his fault, between you and him alone. If he listens to you, you have gained your brother. But if he does not listen, take one or two others along with you, that every charge may be established by the evidence of two or three witnesses. If he refuses to listen to them, tell it to the church. And if he refuses to listen even to the church, let him be to you as a Gentile and a tax collector. Truly, I say to you, whatever you bind on earth shall be bound in heaven, and whatever you loose on earth shall be loosed in heaven. Again I say to you, if two of you agree on earth about anything they ask, it will be done for them by my Father in heaven. For where two or three are gathered in my name, there am I among them. (Matthew 18:15–20)*

> *Now in these days when the disciples were increasing in number, a complaint by the Hellenists arose against the Hebrews because their widows were being neglected in the daily distribution. And the twelve summoned the full number of the disciples and said, "It is not right that we should give up preaching the word of God to serve tables. Therefore, brothers, pick out from among you seven men of good repute, full of the Spirit and of wisdom, whom we will appoint to this duty. But we will devote ourselves to prayer and to the ministry of the word." And what they said pleased the whole gathering, and they chose Stephen, a man full of faith and of the Holy Spirit, and Philip, and Prochorus, and Nicanor, and Timon, and Parmenas, and Nicolaus, a proselyte of Antioch. These they set before the apostles, and they prayed and laid their hands on them. And the word of God continued to increase, and the number of the disciples multiplied greatly in Jerusalem, and a great many of the priests became obedient to the faith. (Acts 6:1–7)*

> *Brothers, if anyone is caught in any transgression, you who are spiritual should restore him in a spirit of gentleness. Keep watch on yourself, lest you too be tempted. Bear one another's burdens, and so fulfill the law of Christ. For if anyone thinks he is something, when he is nothing, he deceives himself. But let each one test his own work, and then his reason to boast will be in himself alone and not in his neighbor. For each will have to bear his own load. (Galatians 6:1–5)*

- We do all of the above in _____ with one another marked by grace, compassion, kindness, humility, meekness, and patience, bearing with one another as the Lord bears with us, and forgiving one another as the Lord forgives us.

> *Put on then, as God's chosen ones, holy and beloved, compassionate hearts, kindness, humility, meekness, and patience, bearing with one another and, if one has a complaint against another, forgiving each other; as the Lord has forgiven you, so you also must forgive. And above all these put on love, which binds everything together in perfect harmony. And let the peace of Christ rule in your hearts, to which indeed you were called in one body. And be thankful. Let the word of Christ dwell in you richly, teaching and admonishing one another in all wisdom, singing psalms and hymns and spiritual songs, with thankfulness in your hearts to God. And whatever you do, in word or deed, do everything in the name of the Lord Jesus, giving thanks to God the Father through him. (Colossians 3:12–17)*

We pray and work as the Lord leads us for justice for all people regardless of race.

> *He has told you, O man, what is good; and what does the LORD require of you but to do justice, and to love kindness, and to walk humbly with your God? (Micah 6:8)*

- We deplore any hierarchy of "race" in the body of Christ or the world around us.

- We celebrate interracial marriages and multi-racial families.

- We train our children to hate racism.

- We work against any injustice that is in any way due to a person's or a people group's "race."

The battle against racism is a _____ battle.

> *Finally, be strong in the Lord and in the strength of his might. Put on the whole armor of God, that you may be able to stand against the schemes of the devil. For we do not wrestle against flesh and blood, but against the rulers, against the authorities, against the cosmic powers over this present darkness, against the spiritual forces of evil in the heavenly places. Therefore take up the whole armor of God, that you may be able to withstand in the evil day, and having done all, to stand firm. (Ephesians 6:10–13)*

- "Race" is more than a social construct; it is a spiritual stronghold.

> *For though we walk in the flesh, we are not waging war according to the flesh. For the weapons of our warfare are not of the flesh but have divine power to destroy strongholds. We destroy arguments and every lofty opinion raised against the knowledge of God, and take every thought captive to obey Christ, being ready to punish every disobedience, when your obedience is complete. (2 Corinthians 10:3–6)*

- Satan is the ultimate agitator behind human discord, and the history and ongoing reality of racism in our world is the outworking of his utter hatred for humanity.

> *We know that we are from God, and the whole world lies in the power of the evil one. (1 John 5:19)*

- The devil and his demons are actively . . .

- Deceiving people into thinking and acting like they are intrinsically superior or inferior to others based upon a sinful perversion of the biblical concept of race.

> *I told you that you would die in your sins, for unless you believe that I am he you will die in your sins.* (John 8:24)

- Trying to destroy individuals and entire groups of people.

> *The thief comes only to steal and kill and destroy. I came that they may have life and have it abundantly.* (John 10:10)

- Attempting to rob people of their God-given dignity and keep people from their God-given rights.

> *And the great dragon was thrown down, that ancient serpent, who is called the devil and Satan, the deceiver of the whole world—he was thrown down to the earth, and his angels were thrown down with him. And I heard a loud voice in heaven, saying, "Now the salvation and the power and the kingdom of our God and the authority of his Christ have come, for the accuser of our brothers has been thrown down, who accuses them day and night before our God."* (Revelation 12:9–10)

- Working to _____ people, especially God's people in the church of Jesus Christ.

> *I appeal to you, brothers, to watch out for those who cause divisions and create obstacles contrary to the doctrine that you have been taught; avoid them. For such persons do not serve our Lord Christ, but their own appetites, and by smooth talk and flattery they deceive the hearts of the naive. For your obedience is known to all, so that I rejoice over you, but I want you to be wise as to what is good and innocent as to what is evil. The God of peace will soon crush Satan under your feet. The grace of our Lord Jesus Christ be with you.* (Romans 16:17–20)

> *Be angry and do not sin; do not let the sun go down on your anger, and give no opportunity to the devil.* (Ephesians 4:26–27)

. . . because we wanted to come to you—I, Paul, again and again—but Satan hindered us. (1 Thessalonians 2:18)

- The battle against racism is a battle against Satan.

> *Anyone whom you forgive, I also forgive. Indeed, what I have forgiven, if I have forgiven anything, has been for your sake in the presence of Christ, so that we would not be outwitted by Satan; for we are not ignorant of his designs.* (2 Corinthians 2:10–11)

The gospel of Jesus Christ is our only _____ in the battle against racism.

> *And you, who were dead in your trespasses and the uncircumcision of your flesh, God made alive together with him, having forgiven us all our trespasses, by canceling the record of debt that stood against us with its legal demands. This he set aside, nailing it to the cross. He disarmed the rulers and authorities and put them to open shame, by triumphing over them in him.* (Colossians 2:13–15)

> *Since therefore the children share in flesh and blood, he himself likewise partook of the same things, that through death he might destroy the one who has the power of death, that is, the devil, and deliver all those who through fear of death were subject to lifelong slavery.* (Hebrews 2:14–15)

- Because of Jesus' life, death, and resurrection . . .
  - Satan has ultimately been defeated.

> *I will put enmity between you and the woman, and between your offspring and her offspring; he shall bruise your head, and you shall bruise his heel.* (Genesis 3:15)

  - Satan will one day be destroyed.

> *Now war arose in heaven, Michael and his angels fighting against the dragon. And the dragon and his angels fought back, but he was defeated, and there was no longer any place for them*

in heaven. And the great dragon was thrown down, that ancient serpent, who is called the devil and Satan, the deceiver of the whole world—he was thrown down to the earth, and his angels were thrown down with him. And I heard a loud voice in heaven, saying, "Now the salvation and the power and the kingdom of our God and the authority of his Christ have come, for the accuser of our brothers has been thrown down, who accuses them day and night before our God. And they have conquered him by the blood of the Lamb and by the word of their testimony, for they loved not their lives even unto death. Therefore, rejoice, O heavens and you who dwell in them! But woe to you, O earth and sea, for the devil has come down to you in great wrath, because he knows that his time is short!" (Revelation 12:7–12)

- All who are in Christ . . .
  - Know Satan's destiny.

    Then I saw an angel coming down from heaven, holding in his hand the key to the bottomless pit and a great chain. And he seized the dragon, that ancient serpent, who is the devil and Satan, and bound him for a thousand years, and threw him into the pit, and shut it and sealed it over him, so that he might not deceive the nations any longer, until the thousand years were ended. After that he must be released for a little while. (Revelation 20:1–3)

  - Embrace our identity.

    Therefore, if anyone is in Christ, he is a new creation. The old has passed away; behold, the new has come. (2 Corinthians 5:17)

    And Jesus came and said to them, "All authority in heaven and on earth has been given to me. Go therefore and make disciples of all nations, baptizing them in the name of the Father and of the Son and of the Holy Spirit, teaching them to observe all that I have commanded you. And behold, I am with you always, to the end of the age." (Matthew 28:18–20)

- We are a diverse family of brothers and sisters . . .
- Joyfully united by the gospel of Jesus Christ . . .
- On a mission to make disciples among all nations.

- As the church . . .
    - We humbly, kindly, lovingly, and confidently lock arms _____.

> *Only let your manner of life be worthy of the gospel of Christ, so that whether I come and see you or am absent, I may hear of you that you are standing firm in one spirit, with one mind striving side by side for the faith of the gospel . . .* (Philippians 1:27)

    - We proclaim the Judge of the world while doing justice in the world.

> *Thus says the LORD: Do justice and righteousness, and deliver from the hand of the oppressor him who has been robbed. And do no wrong or violence to the resident alien, the fatherless, and the widow, nor shed innocent blood in this place.* (Jeremiah 22:3)

> *Therefore be imitators of God, as beloved children.* (Ephesians 5:1)

    - We look forward to the day when Jesus will return and racism will be no more.

> *And they sang a new song, saying, "Worthy are you to take the scroll and to open its seals, for you were slain, and by your blood you ransomed people for God from every tribe and language and people and nation, and you have made them a kingdom and priests to our God, and they shall reign on the earth."* (Revelation 5:9–10)

FOR REFLECTION

What are 1–2 practical steps God may be leading you to take that you are not already taking to address racial injustice in the world?

HUMANITY AND ABORTION

He established a testimony in Jacob and appointed a law in Israel, which he commanded our fathers to teach to their children, that the next generation might know them, the children yet unborn, and arise and tell them to their children, so that they should set their hope in God and not forget the works of God, but keep his commandments . . . (Psalm 78:5–7)

In the United States . . .[28]

• Over __50__ million abortions have occurred since 1973.

• __1__ million abortions occur every year; __90,000__ abortions occur every day; an abortion occurs every 20-25 seconds.

• _____ _____ of American women have an abortion at some point in their lives.

In the world . . .

__50__ million abortions occur every year; __130,000__ abortions occur every day.

• A woman has an abortion almost every __second__ of every __day__.

Abortion and God . . .

For you formed my inward parts; you knitted me together in my mother's womb. I praise you, for I am fearfully and wonderfully made. Wonderful are your works; my soul knows it very well. My frame was not hidden from you, when I was being made in secret, intricately woven in the depths of the earth. Your eyes saw my unformed substance; in your book were written, every one of them, the days

that were formed for me, when as yet there was none of them.
(Psalm 139:13–16)

- Abortion is an affront to God's sovereign authority as _Creator_.

> *Have you not known? Have you not heard? The LORD is the everlasting God, the Creator of the ends of the earth. He does not faint or grow weary; his understanding is unsearchable.*
> (Isaiah 40:28)

  ○ He is the giver of life.

  > *The Spirit of God has made me, and the breath of the Almighty gives me life.* (Job 33:4)

  ○ He is the taker of life.

  > *See now that I, even I, am he, and there is no god beside me; I kill and I make alive; I wound and I heal; and there is none that can deliver out of my hand.* (Deuteronomy 32:39)

- Abortion is an assault on God's _glorious_ work in creation.

> *O LORD, how manifold are your works! In wisdom have you made them all; the earth is full of your creatures.* (Psalm 104:24)

  ○ The way God creates people compels praise.

  > *These all look to you, to give them their food in due season. When you give it to them, they gather it up; when you open your hand, they are filled with good things. When you hide your face, they are dismayed; when you take away their breath, they die and return to their dust. When you send forth your Spirit, they are created, and you renew the face of the ground. May the glory of the LORD endure forever; may the LORD rejoice in his works, who looks on the earth and it trembles, who touches the mountains and they smoke! I will sing to the LORD as long as I live; I will sing praise to my God while I have being. May my*

meditation be pleasing to him, for I rejoice in the LORD.
(Psalm 104:27–34)

- The womb contains a person formed in the image of God.

> *Then God said, "Let us make man in our image, after our likeness. And let them have dominion over the fish of the sea and over the birds of the heavens and over the livestock and over all the earth and over every creeping thing that creeps on the earth." So God created man in his own image, in the image of God he created him; male and female he created them. And God blessed them. And God said to them, "Be fruitful and multiply and fill the earth and subdue it, and have dominion over the fish of the sea and over the birds of the heavens and over every living thing that moves on the earth."* (Genesis 1:26–28)

- If the unborn is not human, no justification for abortion is necessary.
- If the unborn is human, no justification for abortion is adequate.[29]

  - "But women have a right to privacy with their doctors."
  - "But women should have the freedom to choose."
  - "But making abortions illegal forces women to find more dangerous ways to abort their babies."
  - "But more children will create a drain on the economy."

    > "Think of a little girl named Rachel. Rachel is two months old, but she is still six weeks away from being a full-term baby. She was born prematurely at 24 weeks, in the middle of her mother's second trimester. On the day of her birth Rachel weighed one pound, nine ounces, but dropped to just under a pound soon after. She was so small she could rest in the palm of her daddy's hand. She was a tiny, living, human person. Heroic measures were taken to save this child's life. Why? Because

we have an obligation to protect, nurture, and care for other humans who would die without our help—especially little children. Rachel was a vulnerable and valuable human being. But get this . . . if a doctor came into the hospital room and, instead of caring for Rachel, took the life of this little girl as she lay quietly nursing at her mother's breast, it would be homicide. However, if this same little girl—the very same Rachel—was inches away resting inside her mother's womb, she could be legally killed by abortion." – Gregory Koukl[30]

- Though the unborn is visibly hidden from man, he/she is never hidden from God.

> *Your hands fashioned and made me, and now you have destroyed me altogether. Remember that you have made me like clay; and will you return me to the dust. Did you not pour me out like milk and curdle me like cheese? You clothed me with skin and flesh, and knit me together with bones and sinews. You have granted me life and steadfast love, and your care has preserved my spirit. Yet these things you hid in your heart; I know that this was your purpose.* (Job 10:8–13)

○ All of God's works are wonderful.
  - Even (or especially) in the case of _____.

> *As he passed by, he saw a man blind from birth. And his disciples asked him, "Rabbi, who sinned, this man or his parents, that he was born blind?" Jesus answered, "It was not that this man sinned, or his parents, but that the works of God might be displayed in him."* (John 9:1–3)

  - Even (or especially) in the midst of _____.

> *As for you, you meant evil against me, but God meant it for good, to bring it about that many people should be kept alive, as they are today.* (Genesis 50:20)

And we know that for those who love God all things work together for good, for those who are called according to his purpose. For those whom he foreknew he also predestined to be conformed to the image of his Son, in order that he might be the firstborn among many brothers. And those whom he predestined he also called, and those whom he called he also justified, and those whom he justified he also glorified. (Romans 8:28–30)

• What about rape?

> *"Fathers shall not be put to death because of their children, nor shall children be put to death because of their fathers. Each one shall be put to death for his own sin."* (Deuteronomy 24:16)

• What about incest?

> *The book of the genealogy of Jesus Christ, the son of David, the son of Abraham. Abraham was the father of Isaac, and Isaac the father of Jacob, and Jacob the father of Judah and his brothers, and Judah the father of Perez and Zerah by Tamar, and Perez the father of Hezron, and Hezron the father of Ram . . .* (Matthew 1:1–3)

• The message of the gospel: God takes unimaginable evil and turns it into ultimate good.

> *Men of Israel, hear these words: Jesus of Nazareth, a man attested to you by God with mighty works and wonders and signs that God did through him in your midst, as you yourselves know—this Jesus, delivered up according to the definite plan and foreknowledge of God, you crucified and killed by the hands of lawless men. God raised him up, loosing the pangs of death, because it was not possible for him to be held by it.* (Acts 2:22–24)

- Abortion is an attack on God's intimate _____ with the unborn.
  - He fashions them.

    > *Did not he who made me in the womb make him? And did not one fashion us in the womb? (Job 31:15)*

  - He values them.

    > *When men strive together and hit a pregnant woman, so that her children come out, but there is no harm, the one who hit her shall surely be fined, as the woman's husband shall impose on him, and he shall pay as the judges determine. But if there is harm, then you shall pay life for life, eye for eye, tooth for tooth, hand for hand, foot for foot, burn for burn, wound for wound, stripe for stripe. (Exodus 21:22–25)*

  - He knows them.

    > *Before I formed you in the womb I knew you, and before you were born I consecrated you; I appointed you a prophet to the nations. (Jeremiah 1:5)*

  - He relates to them.

    > *Yet you are he who took me from the womb; you made me trust you at my mother's breasts. On you was I cast from my birth, and from my mother's womb you have been my God. (Psalm 22:9–10)*

  - He calls them.

    > *But when he who had set me apart before I was born, and who called me by his grace . . . (Galatians 1:15)*

  - He names them.

    > *Listen to me, O coastlands, and give attention, you peoples from afar. The LORD called me from the womb, from the body of my mother he named my name. (Isaiah 49:1)*

○ He anoints them.

> . . . for he will be great before the Lord. And he must not drink wine or strong drink, and he will be filled with the Holy Spirit, even from his mother's womb (Luke 1:15)

> For behold, when the sound of your greeting came to my ears, the baby in my womb leaped for joy. (Luke 1:44)

Abortion and the Gospel . . .

• God is the Judge of _____.

> Far be it from you to do such a thing, to put the righteous to death with the wicked, so that the righteous fare as the wicked! Far be that from you! Shall not the Judge of all the earth do what is just? (Genesis 18:25)

> He will render to each one according to his works: to those who by patience in well-doing seek for glory and honor and immortality, he will give eternal life; but for those who are self-seeking and do not obey the truth, but obey unrighteousness, there will be wrath and fury. (Romans 2:6–8)

○ Mothers who have aborted babies.
○ Fathers who have encouraged abortion.
○ Grandparents who have supported abortion.
○ Doctors who have performed abortion.
○ Leaders who have permitted abortion.

> Let every person be subject to the governing authorities. For there is no authority except from God, and those that exist have been instituted by God. Therefore whoever resists the authorities resists what God has appointed, and those who resist will incur judgment. For rulers are not a terror to good conduct, but to bad. Would you have no fear of the one who is in authority? Then do what is good, and you will receive his approval, for he

is God's servant for your good. But if you do wrong, be afraid, for he does not bear the sword in vain. For he is the servant of God, an avenger who carries out God's wrath on the wrongdoer. (Romans 13:1–4)

- Government is given by God for the good of people.
- Government is given by God for the _____ of morality.

○ Christians who have done _____ about abortion.

"To endorse or even to be neutral about killing innocent children created in God's image is unthinkable in the Scriptures, was unthinkable to Christians in church history, and should be unthinkable to Christians today." – Randy Alcorn[31]

- God is the Savior of _____.

For we ourselves were once foolish, disobedient, led astray, slaves to various passions and pleasures, passing our days in malice and envy, hated by others and hating one another. But when the goodness and loving kindness of God our Savior appeared, he saved us, not because of works done by us in righteousness, but according to his own mercy, by the washing of regeneration and renewal of the Holy Spirit, whom he poured out on us richly through Jesus Christ our Savior, so that being justified by his grace we might become heirs according to the hope of eternal life. (Titus 3:3–7)

○ He forgives entirely.

For as high as the heavens are above the earth, so great is his steadfast love toward those who fear him; as far as the east is from the west, so far does he remove our transgressions from us. (Psalm 103:11–12)

I, I am he who blots out your transgressions for my own sake, and I will not remember your sins. (Isaiah 43:25)

If we confess our sins, he is faithful and just to forgive us our sins and to cleanse us from all unrighteousness. (1 John 1:9)

- He heals deeply.

  "Therefore I tell you, her sins, which are many, are forgiven—for she loved much. But he who is forgiven little, loves little." And he said to her, "Your sins are forgiven." Then those who were at table with him began to say among themselves, "Who is this, who even forgives sins?" And he said to the woman, "Your faith has saved you; go in peace." (Luke 7:47–50)

- He restores completely.

  There is therefore now no condemnation for those who are in Christ Jesus. (Romans 8:1)

- He redeems fully.

  And we know that for those who love God all things work together for good, for those who are called according to his purpose. (Romans 8:28)

Abortion and the Church . . .

Therefore do not become partners with them; for at one time you were darkness, but now you are light in the Lord. Walk as children of light (for the fruit of light is found in all that is good and right and true), and try to discern what is pleasing to the Lord. Take no part in the unfruitful works of darkness, but instead expose them. (Ephesians 5:7–11)

- Look _____ . . .
  - Learn the facts about abortion.
  - See the pictures of abortion.
  - Understand the reasons behind abortion.
  - Listen to the victims of abortion.

- Step _____ . . .
  - Share your burdens from the past with brothers and/or sisters.
  - Share your struggles in the present with brothers and/or sisters.

- Speak _____ . . .
  - Before God.
  - Before the government.

- Reach _____ . . .
  - Through working for justice in high-risk communities.
  - Through giving to pro-life causes and ministries.
  - Through serving women and men with unwanted pregnancies.
  - Through volunteering at pregnancy centers.
  - Through supporting abortion alternatives.
  - Through fostering or adopting children.
  - Through making disciples.

FOR REFLECTION

What are 1-2 steps God is leading you to take
from the list of actions steps above?

HUMANITY, INFERTILITY, AND ARTIFICIAL REPRODUCTIVE TECHNOLOGY[32]

"... the borderline situation [is] the crucial test of ethics."
– Helmut Thielicke[33]

Foundations for Understanding Infertility . . .

- God designs for children to be conceived in his image through sexual union between a husband and a wife.

  And God blessed them. And God said to them, "Be fruitful and multiply and fill the earth and subdue it, and have dominion over the fish of the sea and over the birds of the heavens and over every living thing that moves on the earth." (Genesis 1:28)

  Therefore a man shall leave his father and his mother and hold fast to his wife, and they shall become one flesh. And the man and his wife were both naked and were not ashamed. (Genesis 2:24–25)

- An unborn child is a human person from the moment of <ins>conception</ins>.

  Behold, I was brought forth in iniquity, and in sin did my mother conceive me. (Psalm 51:5)

  When men strive together and hit a pregnant woman, so that her children come out, but there is no harm, the one who hit her shall surely be fined, as the woman's husband shall impose on him, and he shall pay as the judges determine. But if there is harm, then you shall pay life for life, eye for eye, tooth for tooth, hand for hand, foot for foot, burn for burn, wound for wound, stripe for stripe. (Exodus 21:22–25)

  The children struggled together within her, and she said, "If it is thus, why is this happening to me?" So she went to inquire of the LORD. And the LORD said to her, "Two nations are in your

> womb, and two peoples from within you shall be divided; the
> one shall be stronger than the other, the older shall serve the
> younger." (Genesis 25:22–23)

> For behold, when the sound of your greeting came to my ears,
> the baby in my womb leaped for joy. (Luke 1:44)

- Physical children are a blessing from the Lord.

> He gives the barren woman a home, making her the joyous
> mother of children. Praise the LORD! (Psalm 113:9)

> Behold, children are a heritage from the LORD, the fruit of the
> womb a reward. (Psalm 127:3)

- Spiritual children are a blessing from the Lord.

> "Sing, O barren one, who did not bear; break forth into singing
> and cry aloud, you who have not been in labor! For the children
> of the desolate one will be more than the children of her who is
> married," says the LORD. (Isaiah 54:1)

- Medicine on the whole is a gift from God that is morally good.

> Every good gift and every perfect gift is from above, coming
> down from the Father of lights, with whom there is no variation
> or shadow due to change. (James 1:17)

> Now when the sun was setting, all those who had any who were
> sick with various diseases brought them to him, and he laid his
> hands on every one of them and healed them. (Luke 4:40)

> Is anyone among you sick? Let him call for the elders of the
> church, and let them pray over him, anointing him with oil in the
> name of the Lord. And the prayer of faith will save the one who
> is sick, and the Lord will raise him up. And if he has committed
> sins, he will be forgiven. Therefore, confess your sins to one
> another and pray for one another, that you may be healed. The
> prayer of a righteous person has great power as it is working.
> (James 5:14–16)

- Infertility, the inability to have children through sexual union, is __common__ in the Bible.

> Now Sarai was barren; she had no child. (Genesis 11:30)

> When the LORD saw that Leah was hated, he opened her womb, but Rachel was barren. (Genesis 29:31)

> But they had no child, because Elizabeth was barren, and both were advanced in years. (Luke 1:7)

Encouragement Amidst Infertility . . .

> There was a certain man of Ramathaim-zophim of the hill country of Ephraim whose name was Elkanah the son of Jeroham, son of Elihu, son of Tohu, son of Zuph, an Ephrathite. He had two wives. The name of the one was Hannah, and the name of the other, Peninnah. And Peninnah had children, but Hannah had no children. Now this man used to go up year by year from his city to worship and to sacrifice to the LORD of hosts at Shiloh, where the two sons of Eli, Hophni and Phinehas, were priests of the LORD. On the day when Elkanah sacrificed, he would give portions to Peninnah his wife and to all her sons and daughters. But to Hannah he gave a double portion, because he loved her, though the Lord had closed her womb. And her rival used to provoke her grievously to irritate her, because the LORD had closed her womb. So it went on year by year. As often as she went up to the house of the LORD, she used to provoke her. Therefore Hannah wept and would not eat. And Elkanah, her husband, said to her, "Hannah, why do you weep? And why do you not eat? And why is your heart sad? Am I not more to you than ten sons?" After they had eaten and drunk in Shiloh, Hannah rose. Now Eli the priest was sitting on the seat beside the doorpost of the temple of the Lord. She was deeply distressed and prayed to the LORD and wept bitterly. And she vowed a vow and said, "O LORD of hosts, if you will indeed look on the affliction of your servant and remember me and not forget your servant, but will give to your servant a son, then I will give him to the LORD all the days of his life, and no razor shall touch his head."

As she continued praying before the LORD, Eli observed her mouth. Hannah was speaking in her heart; only her lips moved, and her voice was not heard. Therefore Eli took her to be a drunken woman. And Eli said to her, "How long will you go on being drunk? Put your wine away from you." But Hannah answered, "No, my lord, I am a woman troubled in spirit. I have drunk neither wine nor strong drink, but I have been pouring out my soul before the LORD. Do not regard your servant as a worthless woman, for all along I have been speaking out of my great anxiety and vexation." Then Eli answered, "Go in peace, and the God of Israel grant your petition that you have made to him." And she said, "Let your servant find favor in your eyes." Then the woman went her way and ate, and her face was no longer sad. They rose early in the morning and worshiped before the LORD; then they went back to their house at Ramah. And Elkanah knew Hannah his wife, and the LORD remembered her. And in due time Hannah conceived and bore a son, and she called his name Samuel, for she said, "I have asked for him from the LORD." (1 Samuel 1:1–20)

- Trust in the God who knows the __*mind*__ of your infertility.[34]

> *As for you, you meant evil against me, but God meant it for good, to bring it about that many people should be kept alive, as they are today.* (Genesis 50:20)

- Worship God and treasure him above all things, even a __*baby*__.

> *Three times I pleaded with the Lord about this, that it should leave me. But he said to me, "My grace is sufficient for you, for my power is made perfect in weakness." Therefore I will boast all the more gladly of my weaknesses, so that the power of Christ may rest upon me. For the sake of Christ, then, I am content with weaknesses, insults, hardships, persecutions, and calamities. For when I am weak, then I am strong.* (2 Corinthians 12:8–10)

  ○ The gospel is good news for childless couples who hope in Christ, not in procreation.

> *Indeed, I count everything as loss because of the surpassing worth of knowing Christ Jesus my Lord. For his sake I have suffered the loss of all things and count them as rubbish, in order that I may gain Christ and be found in him, not having a righteousness of my own that comes from the law, but that which comes through faith in Christ, the righteousness from God that depends on faith—that I may know him and the power of his resurrection, and may share his sufferings, becoming like him in his death, that by any means possible I may attain the resurrection from the dead. (Philippians 3:8–11)*

- Pray to God __hopefully__ , persistently, faithfully, and boldly.

> *And he told them a parable to the effect that they ought always to pray and not lose heart. (Luke 18:1)*

- Be honest about your hurt.

> *. . . casting all your anxieties on him, because he cares for you.* (1 Peter 5:7)

- Realize the wide range of experiences and emotions on the __journey__ of infertility.[35]

> *. . . Three things are never satisfied; four never say, "Enough": Sheol, the barren womb, the land never satisfied with water, and the fire that never says, "Enough." (Proverbs 30:15b–16)*

- Hormones
- Expenses
- Decisions
- Anger
- Despair
- Brokenness
- Helplessness
- Sadness
- Feeling uncomfortable at church
- Isolation

- Marital stress
- Family members' pain
- Friends' reactions
- Stories
- Reactions of Christians
- Questioning your faith
- Waiting
- Grief

- Fill your mind with thoughts from __*God*__.

> We destroy arguments and every lofty opinion raised against the knowledge of God, and take every thought captive to obey Christ . . . (2 Corinthians 10:5)

> Finally, brothers, whatever is true, whatever is honorable, whatever is just, whatever is pure, whatever is lovely, whatever is commendable, if there is any excellence, if there is anything worthy of praise, think about these things. What you have learned and received and heard and seen in me—practice these things, and the God of peace will be with you. (Philippians 4:8–9)

- Recognize that God gives limits to humanity for good reason.
  - What is technologically possible is not necessarily morally __*acceptable*__.

- Believe that God ordains difficulties in our lives for __*good*__ purposes.

> And we know that for those who love God all things work together for good, for those who are called according to his purpose. For those whom he foreknew he also predestined to be conformed to the image of his Son, in order that he might be the firstborn among many brothers. And those whom he predestined he also called, and those whom he called he also justified, and those whom he justified he also glorified. (Romans 8:28–30)

Options Amidst Infertility . . .

- Embracing Infertility: A decision to not pursue any of the means of having children below.
  - ○ Biblical Reminder:
    - Embracing infertility according to the leadership of God's Spirit is a beautiful picture of trust in God's sovereign goodness and a powerful testimony to the value of bearing spiritual children.

    > "Sing, O barren one, who did not bear; break forth into singing and cry aloud, you who have not been in labor! For the children of the desolate one will be more than the children of her who is married," says the LORD. (Isaiah 54:1)

- Fertility Medicine and Procedures: Taking medicine or undergoing medical procedures aimed at increasing the _likelihood_ of having a child through sexual union between a husband and wife.
  - ○ Biblical Reminder:
    - Medicine is a good gift from God that is morally good when it accompanies sexual union between a husband and wife.

- Foster Care and Adoption: Legally bringing another's child to raise him or her as a full part of one's _____ either for a period of time (foster care) or for a lifetime (adoption).
  - ○ Traditional Foster Care and Adoption: Occurs after a child is born.
  - ○ Embryo Adoption: Involves a woman carrying another's embryo and giving birth to the child as a full part of one's family.
  - ○ Biblical Reminder:
    - Foster care and adoption are powerful and often painful reflections of the Father's love for the fatherless and the gospel of Jesus Christ.

    > He executes justice for the fatherless and the widow, and loves the sojourner, giving him food and clothing. (Deuteronomy 10:18)

> *Religion that is pure and undefiled before God the Father is this: to visit orphans and widows in their affliction, and to keep oneself unstained from the world. (James 1:27)*
> *When Joseph woke from sleep, he did as the angel of the Lord commanded him: he took his wife, but knew her not until she had given birth to a son. And he called his name Jesus. (Matthew 1:24–25)*

> *For you did not receive the spirit of slavery to fall back into fear, but you have received the Spirit of adoption as sons, by whom we cry, "Abba! Father!" (Romans 8:15)*

> *But when the fullness of time had come, God sent forth his Son, born of woman, born under the law, to redeem those who were under the law, so that we might receive adoption as sons. And because you are sons, God has sent the Spirit of his Son into our hearts, crying, "Abba! Father!" So you are no longer a slave, but a son, and if a son, then an heir through God. (Galatians 4:4–7)*

- Artificial Insemination: The process whereby sperm is artificially placed within a woman so as to make her ___pregnant___.
  - Homologous Insemination: Sperm from the husband in a married couple.
  - Heterologous Insemination: Sperm from a donor.
  - Biblical Concerns:
    - Separates sexual union between a husband and a wife from procreation.
    - Heterologous insemination compromises the unity of marriage.

  - Biblical Reminder:
    - A child conceived through artificial insemination bears the image of God and possesses equal worth before God and others.

- In Vitro Fertilization (IVF): The process of combining sperm and one or more eggs outside a woman's body in a ___laboratory___ for fertilization, then implanting an embryo (or embryos) in a woman's uterus with hopes of her becoming pregnant and having a baby.

- Homologous IVF: Uses sperm and egg from the husband and wife.
- Heterologous IVF: Uses a sperm or egg from someone who is not the husband or wife.
- Biblical Concerns:
  - Separates sexual union between a husband and a wife from procreation.
  - Heterologous IVF compromises the unity of marriage.
  - Introduces selective reduction into the formation of human life.
  - Increases risks for babies and mothers.
  - Often leads to multitudes of embryos'/children's deaths.
  - Opens many opportunities for eugenics and genetic manipulation of embryos.

- Biblical Reminder:
  - A child conceived through artificial insemination bears the image of God and possesses equal worth before God and others.
  - An embryo created through IVF is an unborn child, or a human person made in the image of God.
    - Consider attempting to give birth to this child.
    - Consider allowing this child to be given to a family through adoption.
    - Consider how to work to keep this child from being destroyed, indefinitely frozen, or used for research.
    - If none of the above options are possible, consider allowing this child to go into God's hands with grieving appropriate for death.

- Surrogacy: The practice by which a woman (called a surrogate mother) becomes pregnant and gives birth to a baby in order to give it to someone who cannot (or will not) bear children of their own.

  And Sarai said to Abram, "Behold now, the LORD has prevented me from bearing children. Go in to my servant; it may be that I shall obtain children by her." And Abram listened to the voice of Sarai. (Genesis 16:2)

Then she said, "Here is my servant Bilhah; go in to her, so that she may give birth on my behalf, that even I may have children through her." (Genesis 30:3)

○ Traditional Surrogacy: A surrogate mother is impregnated naturally or artificially, but the resulting child is genetically related to the surrogate mother.
○ Gestational Surrogacy: The pregnancy results from the transfer of an embryo created by in vitro fertilization (IVF), in a manner such that the resulting child is not genetically related to the surrogate.
○ Rescue Surrogacy: A surrogate mother volunteers her womb to save an IVF-created embryo that has been frozen and is destined for destruction.
○ Biblical Concerns:
  ▪ Can violate the covenant of marriage.
  ▪ Separates sexual union between a husband and a wife from procreation.
  ▪ Leads to the exploitation of women.
  ▪ Leads to the selling of children.
  ▪ Increases risks for babies and mothers.
  ▪ Often leads to multitudes of embryos'/children's deaths.
  ▪ Opens many opportunities for eugenics and genetic manipulation of embryos.

FOR REFLECTION

Which options above do you believe are biblically appropriate amidst infertility?

HUMANITY, GENOMICS, AND EUGENICS[36]

Recent Revolutions . . .

- The Atom
- The Bit
- The _____

Terms and Definitions . . .

- Genome: An organism's complete set of _____, including all of its genes. (In humans, a copy of the entire genome—more than 3 billion DNA base pairs—is contained in all cells that have a nucleus.)
  - Genome Editing (Gene Editing): A form of genome engineering in which DNA is inserted, replaced, or removed from the genetic material of a cell using artificially engineered enzymes, or "molecular scissors."[37]
  - CRISPR (CRISPR/Cas9 Genetic Scissors): A technology that enables geneticists and medical researchers to edit the genome of plants, animals, and humans.[38]

> "For billions of years, life progressed according to Darwin's theory of evolution: random mutation in DNA, selection and reproduction. Today, human [sic] meet great challenge when the industrialization has caused great environment change. Genome sequencing and genome editing provided new powerful tools to control evolution. In our lab, we work hard to develop single molecule sequencing platform to read the genetic code of life. We aim to bring down the whole genome sequencing to the goal of $100, and make it available to everyone. As long as the genetic code is known, we use CRISPR-Cas9 to insert, edit or delete the associated gene for a particular trait. By correcting the disease genes, gaining protective alleles, we human [sic] can better live in the fast changing environment." – Lab of He Jiankui[39]

- Human Germ Line: A term used either to refer to sex cells that are passed on from generation to generation or to the lineage of cells spanning generations of individuals.[40]
- Germline Editing: When genome editing is used on the genome of germline cells.

- Eugenics: The practice of _____ the genetic composition of a population by increasing the number of people who have a more desirable trait and reducing the number of people with less desirable traits.
  - Positive Eugenics: Attempts to promote the proliferation of "good stock."
  - Negative Eugenics: Attempts to discourage the continuation of "defective stock."[41]

Categories of Gene Editing . . .

- Therapy (Preventions and Treatments): Efforts to _____ patient genomes with the goal of preventing, stopping, or reversing various diseases or disorders.
- Enhancements: Attempts to edit patient genomes with the goal of _____ capability according to our current understanding of humanity.
- Super-Enhancements: Attempts to edit patient genomes with the goal of increasing capabilities _____ our current understanding of humanity (i.e., capabilities that humans have not had before).

> "Man has the opportunity to get into the genetic code created by either nature, or as religious people would say, by God. One may imagine that scientists could create a person with desired features. This may be a mathematical genius, an outstanding musician, but this can also be a soldier, a person who can fight without fear or compassion, mercy or pain." – Vladimir Putin[42]

- Absolute Improvements: Improvements that are beneficial to you even if _____ else gets them.
- Positional Improvements: Improvements that are beneficial to you if everyone else does _____ get them.

Concerns and Questions with Gene Editing . . .

- Technical concerns and questions include . . .
    - Is this technology being used for therapy or enhancement? How will we use this technology to promote genetic enhancements/improvements and change non-medically relevant characteristics?
    - Where do you draw the _____ between therapy and enhancement?
    - Who is able to make and carry out these determinations?

> "People are already editing human cells using a $150 inverted microscope. . . . The requirements of embryo injection are minimal: a micro-injector, micropipette, and microscope. All of these can be purchased on eBay and assembled for a few thousand dollars. . . . You can probably have the embryo transferred to a human by a medical doctor in the U.S. if you don't tell him or her what you've done, or you can do it in another country. . . . So it won't be long until the next human embryo is edited and implanted. . . . If I could have my children be less prone to being obese or having genes that make them perform better athletically and stuff, why would I say no?" – Josiah Zayner[43]

> "The issue is one of the most profound we humans have ever faced. For the first time in the evolution of life on this planet, a species has developed the capacity to edit its own genetic makeup. That offers the potential of wondrous benefits, including the elimination of many deadly diseases and debilitating abnormalities. And it will someday offer both the promise and the peril of allowing us, or some of us, to boost our bodies and enhance our babies to have better muscles, minds, memory, and moods. In the upcoming decades, as we gain more power to hack our own evolution, we will have to wrestle with deep moral and spiritual questions: Is there an inherent goodness to nature? Is there a virtue that arises from accepting what is gifted to us? Does empathy depend on believing that but for the grace of God, or the randomness of the natural lottery, we could have been born with a different set of endowments? Will an emphasis on personal liberty turn the most fundamental aspects of human

nature into consumer choices made at a genetic supermarket? Should the rich be able to buy the best genes? Should we leave such decisions to individual choice, or should society come to some consensus about what it will allow?" – Walter Isaacson[44]

○ Is this technology being used only on somatic cells (which are non-reproductive and would only affect the individual being treated) or germline cells (which are reproductive cells that could potentially affect future generations)?

- Biblical concerns and questions include . . .
  ○ To what extent are we assuming we can "_____" on God's natural design of the human body?

  > "If scientists don't play God, who will?" – James Watson, to Britain's Parliamentary and Scientific Committee, May 16, 2000

  > "Another reason we might feel uncomfortable with directing our evolution and designing our babies is that we would be 'playing God.' Like Prometheus snatching fire, we would be usurping a power that properly resides above our pay grade. In so doing, we'd lose a sense of humility about our place in Creation."
  > – Walter Isaacson[45]

  ○ To what extent should we _____ babies?

  > "So what do we say to parents who want to use gene editing to produce bigger, more muscular kids with greater stamina? Ones who can run marathons, break tackles, and bend steel with their bare hands? And what does that do to our concept of athletics? Do we go from admiring the diligence of the athlete to admiring instead the wizardry of their genetic engineers? It's easy to put an asterisk next to the home run tallies of José Canseco or Mark McGwire when they admit that they were on steroids. But what do we do if athletes' extra muscles come from genes they were born with? And does it matter if those genes were paid for by their parents rather than bestowed by a random natural lottery?"
  > – Walter Isaacson[46]

> "One odd result of allowing super-enhancements could be that
> children will become like iPhones: a new version will come out
> every few years with better features and apps. Will children as
> they age feel that they are becoming obsolete? That their eyes
> don't have the cool triple-lens enhancements that are engineered
> into the latest version of kids? Fortunately, these are questions
> we can ask for amusement but not for an answer. It will be up to
> our grandchildren to figure these out." – Walter Isaacson[47]

o What will be the effect on future generations, and what decisions
are appropriate for us to make for them?

> "Evolution has been working toward optimizing the human
> genome for 3.85 billion years. Do we really think that some small
> group of human genome tinkerers could do better without all
> sorts of unintended consequences?" – Francis Collins, Director
> of the National Institutes of Health[48]

o Will gene editing lead to unjust forms of inequality? Will discrim-
ination increase for those who are unable or unwilling to modify
their children?

> "In a society that values individual freedom above all else, it
> is hard to find any legitimate basis for restricting the use of
> reprogenetics. . . . If democratic societies allow parents to buy
> environmental advantages for their children, how can they
> prohibit them from buying genetic advantages? Americans
> would respond to any attempt at a ban with the question, 'Why
> can't I give my child beneficial genes that other children get
> naturally?'." – Lee Silver[49]

o What will we _____ in humanity (individually and
altogether) in the process of trying to improve humanity?

> "At this point in our deliberations, we have to face the potential
> conflict between what is desired by the individual versus what is
> good for human civilization. A reduction in mood disorders would
> be seen as a benefit by most of the afflicted individuals, parents,

and families. They would desire it. But does the issue look different when asked from society's vantage point? As we learn to treat mood disorders with drugs and eventually with genetic editing, will we have more happiness but fewer Hemingways? Do we wish to live in a world in which there are no Van Goghs? This question of engineering away mood disorders gets to an even more fundamental question: What is the aim or purpose of life? Is it happiness? Contentment? Lack of pain or bad moods? If so, that may be easy. Or does the good life have aims that are deeper? Should the goal be that each person can flourish, in a more profound fashion, by using talents and traits in a way that is truly fulfilling? If so, that would require authentic experiences, real accomplishments, and true efforts, rather than engineered ones. Does the good life entail making a contribution to our community, society, and civilization? Has evolution encoded such goals into human nature? That might entail sacrifice, pain, mental discomforts, and challenges that we would not always choose."
– Walter Isaacson[50]

Biblical Exhortations in a World of Gene Editing . . .

The proverbs of Solomon, son of David, king of Israel: To know wisdom and instruction, to understand words of insight, to receive instruction in wise dealing, in righteousness, justice, and equity; to give prudence to the simple, knowledge and discretion to the youth—Let the wise hear and increase in learning, and the one who understands obtain guidance, to understand a proverb and a saying, the words of the wise and their riddles. The fear of the LORD is the beginning of knowledge; fools despise wisdom and instruction. (Proverbs 1:1-7)

• Fear God _____.

• Think and act _____.

"Now let's deal with the final frontier, the one most promising and frightful: the possibility of improving cognitive skills such as memory, focus, information processing, and perhaps even

someday the vaguely defined concept of intelligence. Unlike height, cognitive skills are beneficial in more than just a positional way. If everyone were a bit smarter, it probably would make all of us better off. In fact, even if only a portion of the population became smarter, it might benefit everyone in society. Perhaps we will be able to improve our cognitive skills so that we can keep up with the challenges of using our technology wisely. Ah, but there's the rub: wisely. Of all the complex components that go into human intelligence, wisdom may be the most elusive. Understanding the genetic components of wisdom may require us to understand consciousness, and I suspect that's not going to happen in this century. In the meantime, we will have to deploy the finite allocation of wisdom that nature has dealt us as we ponder how to use the gene-editing techniques that we've discovered. Ingenuity without wisdom is dangerous."
– Walter Isaacson[51]

- Study and work _____.

- _____ God completely.

"After millions of centuries during which the evolution of organisms happened 'naturally,' we humans now have the ability to hack the code of life and engineer our own genetic future. Or, to flummox those who would label gene editing as 'unnatural' and 'playing God,' let's put it another way: Nature and nature's God, in their infinite wisdom, have evolved a species that is able to modify its own genome, and that species happens to be ours." – Walter Issacson[52]

Why do the nations rage and the peoples plot in vain? The kings of the earth set themselves, and the rulers take counsel together, against the LORD and against his Anointed, saying, "Let us burst their bonds apart and cast away their cords from us." He who sits in the heavens laughs; the Lord holds them in derision. Then he will speak to them in his wrath, and terrify them in his fury, saying, "As for me, I have set my King on Zion, my holy hill." I will tell of the decree: The LORD said to me, "You are my Son; today

I have begotten you. Ask of me, and I will make the nations your heritage, and the ends of the earth your possession. You shall break them with a rod of iron and dash them in pieces like a potter's vessel." Now therefore, O kings, be wise; be warned, O rulers of the earth. Serve the LORD with fear, and rejoice with trembling. Kiss the Son, lest he be angry, and you perish in the way, for his wrath is quickly kindled. Blessed are all who take refuge in him. (Psalm 2:1–12)

FOR REFLECTION

Which of the following potential uses of gene editing would you support based upon biblical foundations for humanity?

Helping people be less susceptible to deadly viruses?
Eliminating Huntington's disease, sickle cell anemia, and cystic fibrosis?
Preventing blindness or deafness?
Preventing mental or emotional or even learning disorders?
Determining gender? Or sexual inclinations?
Determining skin color? Eye color? Height?
Enhancing cognitive abilities?
Enhancing physical abilities?

HUMANITY AND ARTIFICIAL INTELLIGENCE[53]

"So it is a truly wonderful thing that although man is twisted and corrupted and lost as a result of the Fall, yet he is still man. He has become neither a machine nor an animal nor a plant. The marks of mannishness are still upon him—love, rationality, longing for significance, fear of nonbeing, and so on. This is the case even when his non-Christian system leads him to say these things do not exist. It is these things which distinguish him from the animal and plant world and from the machine." – Francis Schaeffer[54]

Terms and Definitions . . .

- Artificial Intelligence: Non-biological intelligence involving a _____ programmed to accomplish complex goals.[55]
    - Artificial General Intelligence: Human-level artificial intelligence.
    - Artificial Super Intelligence: Beyond (and perhaps way beyond) human-level artificial intelligence.

- Transhumanism: A movement whose aim is to transform humanity by improving human intelligence, physical strength, and the five senses by technological means.

    > *"The human species can, if it wishes, transcend itself—not just sporadically, an individual here in one way, an individual there in another way, but in its entirety, as humanity."* – Julian Huxley[56]

    - One ultimate goal . . .
        - Posthumanism.

    - Two fundamental principles . . .
        - Humanity can _____ our own humanity.
        - Each individual has the fundamental _____ to pursue these enhancements.

    - Three primary waves . . .

- Morphological freedom to change ourselves.
- The use of augmented reality to merge the physical and digital world.
- The pursuit of artificial intelligence to finally transcend our human limitations entirely.

> "The development of full artificial intelligence could spell the end of the human race. . . . It would take off on its own, and re-design itself at an ever increasing rate. Humans, who are limited by slow biological evolution, couldn't compete, and would be superseded." – Stephen Hawking[57]

Questions . . .

- What is the difference between a human and a machine?

- Do machines have rights?

- What are the dangers associated with adding components of machines to human development?

- What moral code should legislate the development of AI?

- Who is responsible for the control of AI?

- What role should AI systems have in government, military, and business applications? To what extent should AI be used in war? To what extent should AI be used to gain advantages in business?

- To what extent will AI eliminate (or create) human jobs?

Biblical Foundations . . .

[The following is a statement of principles developed by the Ethics and Religious Liberty Commission. It is available at erlc.com.[58]]

- Article 1: Image of God
  - We affirm that God created each human being in His image with intrinsic and equal worth, dignity, and moral agency, distinct from all creation, and that humanity's creativity is intended to reflect God's creative pattern.
  - We deny that any part of creation, including any form of technology, should ever be used to usurp or subvert the dominion and stewardship which has been entrusted solely to humanity by God; nor should technology be assigned a level of _____ identity, worth, dignity, or moral agency.

  > *This is the book of the generations of Adam. When God created man, he made him in the likeness of God. Male and female he created them, and he blessed them and named them Man when they were created.* (Genesis 5:1–2)

- Article 2: AI as Technology
  - We affirm that the development of AI is a demonstration of the unique creative abilities of human beings. When AI is employed in accordance with God's moral will, it is an example of man's obedience to the divine command to steward creation and to honor Him. We believe in innovation for the glory of God, the sake of human flourishing, and the love of neighbor. While we acknowledge the reality of the Fall and its consequences on human nature and human innovation, technology can be used in society to uphold human dignity. As a part of our God-given creative nature, human beings should develop and harness technology in ways that lead to greater flourishing and the alleviation of human suffering.
  - We deny that the use of AI is morally _____. It is not worthy of man's hope, worship, or love. Since the Lord Jesus alone can atone for sin and reconcile humanity to its Creator, technology such as AI cannot fulfill humanity's ultimate needs. We further deny the goodness and benefit of any application of AI that devalues or degrades the dignity and worth of another human being.

  > *You shall have no other gods before me.* (Exodus 20:3)

The LORD said to Moses, "See, I have called by name Bezalel the son of Uri, son of Hur, of the tribe of Judah, and I have filled him with the Spirit of God, with ability and intelligence, with knowledge and all craftsmanship, to devise artistic designs, to work in gold, silver, and bronze, in cutting stones for setting, and in carving wood, to work in every craft. And behold, I have appointed with him Oholiab, the son of Ahisamach, of the tribe of Dan. And I have given to all able men ability, that they may make all that I have commanded you: the tent of meeting, and the ark of the testimony, and the mercy seat that is on it, and all the furnishings of the tent, the table and its utensils, and the pure lampstand with all its utensils, and the altar of incense, and the altar of burnt offering with all its utensils, and the basin and its stand, and the finely worked garments, the holy garments for Aaron the priest and the garments of his sons, for their service as priests, and the anointing oil and the fragrant incense for the Holy Place. According to all that I have commanded you, they shall do." (Exodus 31:1–11)

The LORD has made everything for its purpose, even the wicked for the day of trouble. (Proverbs 16:4)

And he said to him, "You shall love the Lord your God with all your heart and with all your soul and with all your mind. This is the great and first commandment. And a second is like it: You shall love your neighbor as yourself. On these two commandments depend all the Law and the Prophets." (Matthew 22:37–40)

. . . for all have sinned and fall short of the glory of God . . . (Romans 3:23)

- Article 3: Relationship of AI & Humanity
  - We affirm the use of AI to inform and aid human reasoning and moral decision-making because it is a tool that excels at processing data and making determinations, which often mimics or exceeds human ability. While AI excels in data-based computation, technology is incapable of possessing the capacity for moral agency or responsibility.

○ We deny that humans can or should cede our moral
_____ or responsibilities to any form
of AI that will ever be created. Only humanity will be judged by
God on the basis of our actions and that of the tools we create.
While technology can be created with a moral use in view, it is
not a moral agent. Humans alone bear the responsibility for moral
decision-making.

> He will render to each one according to his works: to those who
> by patience in well-doing seek for glory and honor and immortality,
> he will give eternal life; but for those who are self-seeking and do
> not obey the truth, but obey unrighteousness, there will be wrath
> and fury. (Romans 2:6–8)

• Article 4: Medicine
    ○ We affirm that AI-related advances in medical technologies are
    expressions of God's common grace through and for people
    created in His image and that these advances will increase our
    capacity to provide enhanced medical diagnostics and therapeutic
    interventions as we seek to care for all people. These advances
    should be guided by basic principles of medical ethics, including
    beneficence, non-maleficence, autonomy, and justice, which are
    all consistent with the biblical principle of loving our neighbor.
    ○ We deny that death and disease—effects of the Fall—can ultimately
    be eradicated apart from _____ _____.
    Utilitarian applications regarding healthcare distribution should
    not override the dignity of human life. Furthermore, we reject
    the materialist and consequentialist worldview that understands
    medical applications of AI as a means of improving, changing, or
    completing human beings.

> Jesus said to her, "I am the resurrection and the life. Whoever
> believes in me, though he die, yet shall he live, and everyone who
> lives and believes in me shall never die. Do you believe this?"
> (John 11:25–26)

> "O death, where is your victory? O death, where is your sting?"
> The sting of death is sin, and the power of sin is the law. But

thanks be to God, who gives us the victory through our Lord Jesus Christ. (1 Corinthians 15:55–57)

Bear one another's burdens, and so fulfill the law of Christ. (Galatians 6:2)

Let each of you look not only to his own interests, but also to the interests of others. (Philippians 2:4)

- Article 5: Bias
  - We affirm that, as a tool created by humans, AI will be inherently subject to bias and that these biases must be accounted for, minimized, or removed through continual human oversight and discretion. AI should be designed and used in such ways that treat all human beings as having equal worth and dignity. AI should be utilized as a tool to identify and eliminate bias inherent in human decision-making.
  - We deny that AI should be designed or used in ways that violate the fundamental principle of human dignity for _____ people. Neither should AI be used in ways that reinforce or further any ideology or agenda, seeking to subjugate human autonomy under the power of the state.

    He has told you, O man, what is good; and what does the LORD require of you but to do justice, and to love kindness, and to walk humbly with your God? (Micah 6:8)

    A new commandment I give to you, that you love one another: just as I have loved you, you also are to love one another. (John 13:34)

- Article 6: Sexuality
  - We affirm the goodness of God's design for human sexuality which prescribes the sexual union to be an exclusive relationship between a man and a woman in the lifelong covenant of marriage.
  - We deny that the pursuit of sexual pleasure is a justification for the development or use of AI, and we condemn the objectification of humans that results from employing AI for

sexual purposes. AI should not intrude upon or substitute for the biblical expression of _____ between a husband and wife according to God's design for human marriage.

> *Therefore a man shall leave his father and his mother and hold fast to his wife, and they shall become one flesh. And the man and his wife were both naked and were not ashamed.* (Genesis 2:24–25)

> *For this is the will of God, your sanctification: that you abstain from sexual immorality; that each one of you know how to control his own body in holiness and honor . . .* (1 Thessalonians 4:3–4)

- Article 7: Work
  - We affirm that work is part of God's plan for human beings participating in the cultivation and stewardship of creation. The divine pattern is one of labor and rest in healthy proportion to each other. Our view of work should not be confined to commercial activity; it must also include the many ways that human beings serve each other through their efforts. AI can be used in ways that aid our work or allow us to make fuller use of our gifts. The church has a Spirit-empowered responsibility to help care for those who lose jobs and to encourage individuals, communities, employers, and governments to find ways to invest in the development of human beings and continue making vocational contributions to our lives together.
  - We deny that human worth and dignity is reducible to an individual's economic contributions to society alone. Humanity should not use AI and other technological innovations as a reason to move toward lives of pure _____ even if greater social wealth creates such possibilities.

> *The LORD God took the man and put him in the garden of Eden to work it and keep it.* (Genesis 2:15)

> *They shall build houses and inhabit them; they shall plant vineyards and eat their fruit. They shall not build and another*

inhabit; they shall not plant and another eat; for like the days of a tree shall the days of my people be, and my chosen shall long enjoy the work of their hands. They shall not labor in vain or bear children for calamity, for they shall be the offspring of the blessed of the Lord, and their descendants with them. Before they call I will answer; while they are yet speaking I will hear. (Isaiah 65:21–24)

- Article 8: Data & Privacy
  - We affirm that privacy and personal property are intertwined individual rights and choices that should not be violated by governments, corporations, nation-states, and other groups, even in the pursuit of the common good. While God knows all things, it is neither wise nor obligatory to have every detail of one's life open to society.
  - We deny the manipulative and coercive uses of data and AI in ways that are _____ with the love of God and love of neighbor. Data collection practices should conform to ethical guidelines that uphold the dignity of all people. We further deny that consent, even informed consent, although requisite, is the only necessary ethical standard for the collection, manipulation, or exploitation of personal data—individually or in the aggregate. AI should not be employed in ways that distort truth through the use of generative applications. Data should not be mishandled, misused, or abused for sinful purposes to reinforce bias, strengthen the powerful, or demean the weak.

You shall not steal. (Exodus 20:15)

Great is our Lord, and abundant in power; his understanding is beyond measure. (Psalm 147:5)

For the word of God is living and active, sharper than any two-edged sword, piercing to the division of soul and of spirit, of joints and of marrow, and discerning the thoughts and intentions of the heart. And no creature is hidden from his sight, but all are naked and exposed to the eyes of him to whom we must give account. (Hebrews 4:12–13)

Article 9: Security

- ○ We affirm that AI has legitimate applications in policing, intelligence, surveillance, investigation, and other uses supporting the government's responsibility to respect human rights, to protect and preserve human life, and to pursue justice in a flourishing society.
- ○ We deny that AI should be employed for safety and security applications in ways that seek to dehumanize, depersonalize, or harm our fellow human beings. We condemn the use of AI to suppress free expression or other basic human _____ granted by God to all human beings.

> Be subject for the Lord's sake to every human institution, whether it be to the emperor as supreme, or to governors as sent by him to punish those who do evil and to praise those who do good. (1 Peter 2:13–14)

- Article 10: War
  - ○ We affirm that the use of AI in warfare should be governed by love of neighbor and the principles of just war. The use of AI may mitigate the loss of human life, provide greater protection of non-combatants, and inform better policymaking. Any lethal action conducted or substantially enabled by AI must employ human oversight or review. All defense-related AI applications, such as underlying data and decision-making processes, must be subject to continual review by legitimate authorities. When these systems are deployed, human agents bear full moral responsibility for any actions taken by the system.
  - ○ We deny that human agency or moral culpability in _____ can be delegated to AI. No nation or group has the right to use AI to carry out genocide, terrorism, torture, or other war crimes.

> And the LORD said, "What have you done? The voice of your brother's blood is crying to me from the ground." (Genesis 4:10)

> . . . for he is God's servant for your good. But if you do wrong, be afraid, for he does not bear the sword in vain. For he is the servant of God, an avenger who carries out God's wrath on the wrongdoer. (Romans 13:4)

- Article 11: Public Policy
  - We affirm that the fundamental purposes of government are to protect human beings from harm, punish those who do evil, uphold civil liberties, and to commend those who do good. The public has a role in shaping and crafting policies concerning the use of AI in society, and these decisions should not be left to those who develop these technologies or to governments to set norms.
  - We deny that AI should be used by governments, corporations, or any entity to infringe upon God-given human rights. AI, even in a highly advanced state, should never be delegated the governing _____ that has been granted by an all-sovereign God to human beings alone.

> Let every person be subject to the governing authorities. For there is no authority except from God, and those that exist have been instituted by God. Therefore whoever resists the authorities resists what God has appointed, and those who resist will incur judgment. For rulers are not a terror to good conduct, but to bad. Would you have no fear of the one who is in authority? Then do what is good, and you will receive his approval, for he is God's servant for your good. But if you do wrong, be afraid, for he does not bear the sword in vain. For he is the servant of God, an avenger who carries out God's wrath on the wrongdoer. Therefore one must be in subjection, not only to avoid God's wrath but also for the sake of conscience. For because of this you also pay taxes, for the authorities are ministers of God, attending to this very thing. Pay to all what is owed to them: taxes to whom taxes are owed, revenue to whom revenue is owed, respect to whom respect is owed, honor to whom honor is owed. (Romans 13:1–7)

- Article 12: The Future of AI
  - We affirm that AI will continue to be developed in ways that we cannot currently imagine or understand, including AI that will far surpass many human abilities. God alone has the power to create life, and no future advancements in AI will usurp Him as the Creator of life. The church has a unique role in proclaiming human dignity for all and calling for the humane use of AI in all aspects of society.

○ We deny that AI will make us more or less human, or that AI will ever obtain a _____ level of worth, dignity, or value to image-bearers. Future advancements in AI will not ultimately fulfill our longings for a perfect world. While we are not able to comprehend or know the future, we do not fear what is to come because we know that God is omniscient and that nothing we create will be able to thwart His redemptive plan for creation or to supplant humanity as His image-bearers.

> *In the beginning, God created the heavens and the earth.* (Genesis 1:1)

> *I am the LORD; that is my name; my glory I give to no other, nor my praise to carved idols.* (Isaiah 42:8)

FOR REFLECTION

If someone were to ask you to explain the primary differences between humans and machines, and why those differences are significant, how would you respond?

HUMANITY, DIGITAL AND SOCIAL MEDIA, AND THE METAVERSE[59]

Terms and Definitions . . .

- _____ Media: Video, audio, software, or other content that is created, edited, stored, or accessed in digital form, through numeric encoding and decoding of data.[60]

- _____ Media: Forms of electronic communication through which users create online communities to share information, ideas, personal messages, and other content (such as videos).[61]

- _____: The metaverse is a "massively-scaled and interoperable network of real-time rendered 3D virtual worlds which can be experienced synchronously and persistently by an effectively unlimited number of users, and with continuity of data, such as identity, history, entitlements, objects, communications, and payments."[62]
    - "A digital world of worlds through which people can travel seamlessly, retaining their appearance and digital possessions wherever they go."[63]
    - These worlds do not merely exist in VR (virtual reality), but also layer onto physical reality through AR (augmented reality).

    > " . . . the feeling of presence [is] the defining quality of the metaverse. You're going to really feel like you're there with other people. You'll see their facial expressions, you'll see their body language . . . all the subtle ways we communicate that today's technology can't quite deliver." – Mark Zuckerberg[64]

- _____ Reality: An artificial environment which is experienced through sensory stimuli (such as sights and sounds) provided by a computer and in which one's actions partially determine what happens in the environment.[65]

- _____ Reality: An enhanced version of reality created by the use of technology to overlay digital information on an image of something being viewed through a device.[66]

Biblical Exhortations . . .

1. **Trust that the Imago Dei will always be _____ than the Imago Meta (or Imago Anything Else).** Our highest dignity and greatest joy is found in the identity we have received from God, and no identity customized by us can ever come close to it. In fact, identities customized by us can rob us of the dignity and joy that our Creator has lovingly, carefully, and personally designed for us. We would be wise to see ourselves, and others, as they have been made by God, not as they are projected through social media or the metaverse.

> Then God said, "Let us make man in our image, after our likeness. And let them have dominion over the fish of the sea and over the birds of the heavens and over the livestock and over all the earth and over every creeping thing that creeps on the earth." (Genesis 1:26)

2. **Insist upon the _____ of our physical bodies, physical relationships, and physical spaces in God's good design for the world.**

> The LORD God took the man and put him in the garden of Eden to work it and keep it. (Genesis 2:15)

> Therefore a man shall leave his father and his mother and hold fast to his wife, and they shall become one flesh. And the man and his wife were both naked and were not ashamed. (Genesis 2:24–25)

3. **Proceed with extreme _____.** The negative effects of digital and social media are well-documented, both for those who post and for those who consume. Digital and social media often lead to addiction on various levels; the spread of misinformation; the distortion of news; mental, physical, emotional, financial, and other manipulation; increased anxiety, stress, depression, and loneliness; decreased productivity; lower attention spans; diminished listening and critical thinking skills; damaged personal relationships; unhealthy sleep and rest patterns . . . and the list could go on and on. For all

these reasons and more, seriously consider limiting (and in various ways completely avoiding) the use of digital and social media in your life. Be wise in every way possible—guarding your heart, mind, and speech in relation to digital and social media.

> *The discerning sets his face toward wisdom, but the eyes of a fool are on the ends of the earth.* (Proverbs 17:24)

> *A fool gives full vent to his spirit, but a wise man quietly holds it back.* (Proverbs 29:11)

> *Look carefully then how you walk, not as unwise but as wise, making the best use of the time, because the days are evil. Therefore do not be foolish, but understand what the will of the Lord is.* (Ephesians 5:15–17)

4. **Fear God.** Let everything you see, say, or do on digital and social media be done in the fear of God.

> *The fear of the LORD is the beginning of knowledge; fools despise wisdom and instruction.* (Proverbs 1:7)

> *The eyes of the LORD are in every place, keeping watch on the evil and the good.* (Proverbs 15:3)

5. **Cultivate beauty, truth, and wonder in what you say and do.** Use digital and social media to celebrate the beauty of God's creation, the presence of his common grace, and the many evidences of his goodness in the world around us. Share how God, his Word, and his work in the world are edifying you in a way that edifies others.

> *You have multiplied, O LORD my God, your wondrous deeds and your thoughts toward us; none can compare with you! I will proclaim and tell of them, yet they are more than can be told.* (Psalm 40:5)

6. **Enjoy and steward opportunities to encourage and connect with other people**. Use digital and social media to encourage and

connect with brothers and sisters in Christ, people who don't yet know Christ, family, friends, and particularly people who you are not able to see or interact with on a regular basis.

> Let the word of Christ dwell in you richly, teaching and admonishing one another in all wisdom, singing psalms and hymns and spiritual songs, with thankfulness in your hearts to God. (Colossians 3:16)

7. _____ and _____ before you speak or act (send or post). Always take appropriate time to consider your words and actions before you say or do anything. And take extra time when you are responding to someone or something else you have seen or heard. Whenever possible, consider waiting 24 hours before responding on digital or social media to anything.

> Whoever despises the word brings destruction on himself, but he who reveres the commandment will be rewarded. (Proverbs 13:3)

> Do you see a man who is hasty in his words? There is more hope for a fool than for him. (Proverbs 29:20)

8. Always ask two questions:

(1) Will what I say or do _____ God? Ask if what you are saying or doing will classify as a good work that brings glory to our Father who is in heaven.

> You are the salt of the earth, but if salt has lost its taste, how shall its saltiness be restored? It is no longer good for anything except to be thrown out and trampled under people's feet. You are the light of the world. A city set on a hill cannot be hidden. Nor do people light a lamp and put it under a basket, but on a stand, and it gives light to all in the house. In the same way, let your light shine before others, so that they may see your good works and give glory to your Father who is in heaven. (Matthew 5:13–16)

(2) Will what I say or do _____ the gospel? Because the gospel of Jesus Christ is of primary importance in each of our lives, ask if what you are saying or doing will reflect positively on the picture people have of the gospel and the life of Jesus in you.

> *At the same time, pray also for us, that God may open to us a door for the word, to declare the mystery of Christ, on account of which I am in prison—that I may make it clear, which is how I ought to speak. Walk in wisdom toward outsiders, making the best use of the time. Let your speech always be gracious, seasoned with salt, so that you may know how you ought to answer each person. (Colossians 4:3–6)*

9. **When in doubt, don't.** When you are uncertain or have hesitations, don't send, post, tweet or retweet, like or dislike, or say or do anything else on digital or social media. This is especially applicable when deeper discussion of an issue is either warranted or wise, when particular nuance is needed around certain ideas or statements, when definitions of words are not clear, or when what you're saying or doing is not clearly and unequivocally biblical and it's likely to cause controversy.

> *When words are many, transgression is not lacking, but whoever restrains his lips is prudent. (Proverbs 10:19)*

10. **Avoid harsh and hurtful speech.** Harsh and hurtful words are always dangerous and destructive, and they're a lot easier to express on digital or social media than in person. Avoid them completely.

> *There is one whose rash words are like sword thrusts, but the tongue of the wise brings healing. (Proverbs 12:18)*

> *A hot-tempered man stirs up strife, but he who is slow to anger quiets contention. (Proverbs 15:18)*

11. **Avoid quarrelsome, retaliatory, and inflammatory speech.** Fools quarrel, especially over texts, emails, and digital and social media outlets. Explore God-glorifying, neighbor-loving ways to engage in meaningful dialogue about myriad disagreements.

A fool's lips walk into a fight, and his mouth invites a beating. (Proverbs 18:6)

It is an honor for a man to keep aloof from strife, but every fool will be quarreling. (Proverbs 20:3)

12. **Avoid gossip and slander**. Make sure that everything you communicate on digital or social media is useful for building up others according to their needs in Christ Jesus. Flee from all gossip and slander in everything you read and communicate to others.

A worthless man plots evil, and his speech is like a scorching fire. A dishonest man spreads strife, and a whisperer separates close friends. (Proverbs 16:27–28)

Let no corrupting talk come out of your mouths, but only such as is good for building up, as fits the occasion, that it may give grace to those who hear. And do not grieve the Holy Spirit of God, by whom you were sealed for the day of redemption. Let all bitterness and wrath and anger and clamor and slander be put away from you, along with all malice. Be kind to one another, tenderhearted, forgiving one another, as God in Christ forgave you. (Ephesians 4:29–32)

13. **Avoid grumbling and complaining**. About anyone or anything.

Do all things without grumbling or disputing, that you may be blameless and innocent, children of God without blemish in the midst of a crooked and twisted generation, among whom you shine as lights in the world . . . (Philippians 2:14–15)

14. **Avoid saying or doing on a screen what you wouldn't say or do in _____**. It is so much easier to do something or say something to or about someone in an email, post, message, text, or in the metaverse that you would not do or say if you were physically with that person. Actually, it's usually cowardly and selfish to do or say such things through digital mediums because we are intentionally avoiding any discomfort we might experience when we do or say

hard things in person. We actually need to see and feel others' physical responses when in these situations. Therefore, avoid actions or conversations over digital or social media that need to take place in person. Even if you conclude for wise and good reasons that something needs to be done or said on digital or social media, still do or say it in person (physically) first. Don't be a lion behind a technological device and a lamb in front of actual people.

> For even if I boast a little too much of our authority, which the Lord gave for building you up and not for destroying you, I will not be ashamed. I do not want to appear to be frightening you with my letters. For they say, "His letters are weighty and strong, but his bodily presence is weak, and his speech of no account." Let such a person understand that what we say by letter when absent, we do when present. (2 Corinthians 10:8–11)

15. **Avoid communicating to "that" person or group of people at "that" time without considering "every" person and group of people at "any" time.** When using digital or social media, we often have a particular audience in mind, including a specific person or group of people at a specific time. However, once we release something into the digital world, it may be observed by far more than "that" person or group of people at any time. Always consider how every person or group of people may perceive what you're saying and how you're saying it at any time (either now or in the future).

> And let us consider how to stir up one another to love and good works . . . (Hebrews 10:24)

16. **Conduct yourself honestly**. Digital and social media can be used as a mask to present a false persona to other people in ways that we start to believe we are that person when we are not. Conduct yourself honestly and resist the temptation to put forward a false image of yourself. This doesn't mean we must share every struggle we experience or all the details of our lives. Some things in our lives are better shared when physically present with people who are close to us.

All the ways of a man are pure in his own eyes, but the LORD weighs the spirit. (Proverbs 16:2)

Therefore do not pronounce judgment before the time, before the Lord comes, who will bring to light the things now hidden in darkness and will disclose the purposes of the heart. Then each one will receive his commendation from God. (1 Corinthians 4:5)

17. **Cultivate** _____. Approach digital and social media with a mindset that says, "Jesus must become greater, and I must become less." By all means, rejoice in God's grace in your life in ways that point to his glory. At the same time, at least be cautious of the humble brag, describing how "humbled" or "grateful" you are to achieve something if you are actually desiring exaltation in others' eyes. Finally, don't base your identity or mood on how many likes or follows or retweets or whatever you have. Our focus on these things exposes our desire for people's approval, while in Christ, we already have the approval of God. Ultimately, use digital and social media to point people to him, not you.

He must increase, but I must decrease. (John 3:30)

When pride comes, then comes disgrace, but with the humble is wisdom. (Proverbs 11:2)

Let another praise you, and not your own mouth; a stranger, and not your own lips. (Proverbs 27:2)

If you have been foolish, exalting yourself, or if you have been devising evil, put your hand on your mouth. (Proverbs 30:32)

18. **Have accountability**. We all need others in our lives who have access to our digital and social media and input into our use of it. Don't have an email, Instagram, Twitter, Facebook, or other account that another brother or sister in Christ cannot access. Consider giving your spouse or another brother or sister in Christ whom you trust access to your accounts. Moreover, if you have any question about something you are seeing or sending or doing, then discuss it with another brother or sister in Christ first. In the end, don't

trust yourself. Instead, trust the Spirit of Jesus in you *and* in other brothers and sisters in Christ around you.

> *Listen to advice and accept instruction, that you may gain wisdom in the future.* (Proverbs 19:20)

> *Cease to hear instruction, my son, and you will stray from the words of knowledge.* (Proverbs 19:27)

> *Iron sharpens iron, and one man sharpens another.* (Proverbs 27:17)

19. **Don't let digital or social media _____ you.** Is your phone a constant pull in your life? Does a quick check of your phone turn into lost time of scrolling and searching? Whenever you have a free minute, do you default to your phone? Are you present in conversations and interactions with family and friends, or are you regularly pulling out your phone to check your digital and social media? Does a notification take precedent over whatever else you are doing in that moment? Resist the control that digital and social media can demand. Instead, walk in step with God's Spirit. Let him be the only one who can speak into your life at any moment, not your phone, Instagram, Twitter, Facebook, email, or any other media outlet.

> *"All things are lawful for me," but not all things are helpful. "All things are lawful for me," but I will not be dominated by anything.* (1 Corinthians 6:12)

20. **Don't let digital or social media _____ you.** More friends, likes, or other affirmations on digital or social media do not mean that you are better known, more social, well liked, or that you have a strong, healthy community filled with meaningful human connections. These indicators in digital and social media can actually mean the opposite, for the use of digital and social media often leads to less meaningful human connections, decreased attention spans, depression, mental instability, and much more.

See to it that no one takes you captive by philosophy and empty deceit, according to human tradition, according to the elemental spirits of the world, and not according to Christ. (Colossians 2:8)

21. Guard your heart from envy, jealousy, pride, and ambition. Digital and social media can be a contentment killer. Observing *this* person who has *that*, or *that* person who has achieved *this*, can subtly, almost unknowingly, start to fuel covetousness, insecurity, and discontentment. This can also cut in prideful ways, fueling thoughts of superiority. In all of this, guard your heart. Rejoice with others who are rejoicing, hurt with others who are hurting, and keep your eyes on Jesus and what he says to and about you.

Keep your heart with all vigilance, for from it flow the springs of life. (Proverbs 4:23)

Do nothing from selfish ambition or conceit, but in humility count others more significant than yourselves. Let each of you look not only to his own interests, but also to the interests of others. (Philippians 2:3–4)

22. Guard your mind from falsehood, filth, and frivolity. Is your use of digital and social media conforming you to the pattern of this world, or transforming you by the renewal of your mind? Make sure that these media outlets are instruments in God's hands for your sanctification, not instruments in the adversary's hands for your destruction. Beware falsehood, including lies about God, others, you, and the world that spread so easily on digital and social media. Beware filth, which is available at your fingertips at every moment of the day. And beware frivolity, filling your mind with an endless drivel of the world that leaves no room for what matters most according to God's Word. Consider wise ways to limit and/or avoid sources of falsehood, filth, and frivolity.

Do not be conformed to this world, but be transformed by the renewal of your mind, that by testing you may discern what is the will of God, what is good and acceptable and perfect. (Romans 12:2)

I will not set before my eyes anything that is worthless. I hate the work of those who fall away; it shall not cling to me. (Psalm 101:3)

Whoever works his land will have plenty of bread, but he who follows worthless pursuits lacks sense. (Proverbs 12:11)

23. **Guard your life from ungodly influences, unhealthy friendships, and unhelpful associations**. Who and what you're doing, seeing, hearing, following, liking, and associating with on digital and social media will inevitably affect you and others' perceptions of you. Personally, influences on social media will either push you toward godliness, healthy relationships, and helpful connections or pull you away from these things. Do not assume that media content has no impact on your life, and do not intentionally or unintentionally yield moral authority in your life to anyone but God and his Word. Even with a healthy desire to be aware of how other people think who believe differently than you, be aware of their influence upon you and others' perception of you (especially as "likes" or "follows" can often be viewed by others as endorsements). Remember that social media is continually influencing and shaping your life as well as the lives of those around you, especially as people are watching and listening to anything you do on digital and social media.

Do not enter the path of the wicked, and do not walk in the way of the evil. Avoid it; do not go on it; turn away from it and pass on. (Proverbs 4:14–15)

One who is righteous is a guide to his neighbor, but the way of the wicked leads them astray. (Proverbs 12:26)

Whoever walks with the wise becomes wise, but the companion of fools will suffer harm. (Proverbs 13:20)

Do not be deceived: "Bad company ruins good morals." (1 Corinthians 15:33)

24. **Flee sexual immorality.** Digital and social media provide countless temptations to sexual immorality, which includes any sexual thinking,

desiring, or acting outside of marriage between a man and a woman. So flee all sexual lust—do not view or send or do anything that provokes sexual immorality in your own life. Flee sexual immodesty—do not say, send, or do anything that might provoke sexual immorality in others. Flee sexual allurement—do not say, send, or do anything that in any way leads to inappropriate physical or emotional attachment. And flee viewing or sending or doing anything that exalts, glamorizes, jokes about, and/or makes light of any kind of sexual immorality.

Flee from sexual immorality. Every other sin a person commits is outside the body, but the sexually immoral person sins against his own body. Or do you not know that your body is a temple of the Holy Spirit within you, whom you have from God? You are not your own, for you were bought with a price. So glorify God in your body. (1 Corinthians 6:18–20)

25. **Be cautious in one-on-one interaction with someone else's spouse**. Don't interact with someone who is married through digital or social media in a way that you would not interact with them with their husband or wife present. In order to be blameless and above reproach, consider appropriate times to include either that person's spouse or another adult. Similarly, if you are married and interacting with someone who is single, avoid interacting in a way that you would not do so with your spouse present.

Therefore, beloved, since you are waiting for these, be diligent to be found by him without spot or blemish, and at peace. (2 Peter 3:14)

26. **Avoid one-on-one interaction with minors**. In order to promote safety for minors (anyone under the age of 18), adults should always seek parental consent before directly interacting with a minor through digital or social media, and then include an adult on that personal interaction with a minor.

Whoever receives one such child in my name receives me, but whoever causes one of these little ones who believe in me to sin, it would be better for him to have a great millstone fastened around his neck and to be drowned in the depth of the sea. (Matthew 18:5–6)

27. Be open, honest, and up-to-date in interaction between minors and parents. Children and teenagers, be open and honest with your parents or guardians about all your interactions online. Parents and guardians, love and serve your children and teenagers by learning about technology, exploring technology with your children and teenagers, introducing them to technology in helpful ways, promoting open communication, providing healthy boundaries, and staying up-to-speed on current technological resources and social trends, apps, lingo, etc.

> *Children, obey your parents in the Lord, for this is right. "Honor your father and mother" (this is the first commandment with a promise), "that it may go well with you and that you may live long in the land." Fathers, do not provoke your children to anger, but bring them up in the discipline and instruction of the Lord.* (Ephesians 6:1–4)

28. Make the _____ of every opportunity. Our lives are a mist in this world, and every moment counts. God has given us the ability to communicate with people around us and around the world through digital and social media, so let's maximize these means at every moment for the glory of God and the spread of his gospel. Let's especially explore the limitless opportunities available for using digital and social media for the spread of the gospel among the unreached.

> *Walk in wisdom toward outsiders, making the best use of the time.* (Colossians 4:5)

> *. . . and thus I make it my ambition to preach the gospel, not where Christ has already been named, lest I build on someone else's foundation . . .* (Romans 15:20)

29. **Make sure not to neglect other _____.** Even
as we leverage digital and social media for good, let's also limit
them for good. Consider other priorities in your life that are more
important. For example, God has created us to work hard for his
glory, and if we're not careful, digital and social media can hinder
our productivity. Or consider God's call for us to rest. How easy it
is for us to think that when we have a free minute, we don't want
to waste it just sitting there, so we might as well look at digital or
social media. But what if God has designed those moments for us
to simply rest our minds and be present in that moment instead of
being preoccupied on a screen? Consider also your time physically
with other people. Don't let digital or social media replace personal,
physical interaction with family, friends, co-workers, neighbors, and
other people God sovereignly brings into your path. Above all,
consider your time alone with God. Scripture calls us to pray
without ceasing, not text or email or post or game without ceasing.
What if prayer was a more automatic reflex in your life than checking
your phone? How might that change not just your prayer life, but
your entire life? Prioritize your time with the God who loves you and
who alone is worthy to be the dominant influence in your life.

> *For we hear that some among you walk in idleness, not busy
> at work, but busybodies. Now such persons we command and
> encourage in the Lord Jesus Christ to do their work quietly and
> to earn their own living.* (2 Thessalonians 3:11–12)

> *It is in vain that you rise up early and go late to rest, eating
> the bread of anxious toil; for he gives to his beloved sleep.*
> (Psalm 127:2)

> *. . . pray without ceasing . . .* (1 Thessalonians 5:17)

30. **Do all to the glory of God.** Many opportunities exist to bring
glory to God through digital and social media, so to paraphrase
1 Corinthians 10:31, "Whether you text, send, post, tweet, or
whatever you do, do all to the glory of God."

So, whether you eat or drink, or whatever you do, do all to the glory of God. (1 Corinthians 10:31)

FOR REFLECTION

Out of all the encouragements listed above, which
2-3 do you need to grow in most?

ULTIMATE
CONCLUSIONS

WHO IS GOD?

"What comes into our minds when we think about God is the most important thing about us." – A.W. Tozer[67]

"The heaviest obligation lying upon the Christian Church today is to purify and elevate her concept of God until it is once more worthy of Him—and of her." – A.W. Tozer[68]

Thus says the LORD: "Let not the wise man boast in his wisdom, let not the mighty man boast in his might, let not the rich man boast in his riches, but let him who boasts boast in this, that he understands and knows me, that I am the LORD who practices steadfast love, justice, and righteousness in the earth. For in these things I delight, declares the LORD." (Jeremiah 9:23–24)

And this is eternal life, that they know you, the only true God, and Jesus Christ whom you have sent. (John 17:3)

The defining characteristic of humanity is the _____ of God.

• Your defining characteristic is that you are made in the image of God.

> *So God created man in his own image, in the image of God he created him; male and female he created them. (Genesis 1:27)*

• Your dignity is not achieved by what you create, but _____ by the One who created you.

> *For you formed my inward parts; you knitted me together in my mother's womb. I praise you, for I am fearfully and wonderfully made. Wonderful are your works; my soul knows it very well. My frame was not hidden from you, when I was being made in secret, intricately woven in the depths of the earth. Your eyes saw my unformed substance; in your book were written, every one of them, the days that were formed for me, when as yet there was none of them. (Psalm 139:13–16)*

> You have given him dominion over the works of your hands; you
> have put all things under his feet . . . (Psalm 8:5)

- Your identity is not found in believing or living "your truth," but in
  believing and living in "the One who is true."

> . . . and you will know the truth, and the truth will set you free.
> (John 8:32)

- Your happiness is not found in self-determination, but in
  self-_____: turning from your sin and yourself to
  trust in Jesus as the Savior and Lord of your life.

> The thief comes only to steal and kill and destroy. I came that
> they may have life and have it abundantly. (John 10:10)

**All of humanity's efforts to reject, rebel against, compete with, or
oppose God are ultimately _____ and futile.**

- God is in no way threatened by any of man's ingenuity or capabilities.

> Behold, the LORD God comes with might, and his arm rules for
> him; behold, his reward is with him, and his recompense before
> him. He will tend his flock like a shepherd; he will gather the
> lambs in his arms; he will carry them in his bosom, and gently
> lead those that are with young. Who has measured the waters
> in the hollow of his hand and marked off the heavens with a
> span, enclosed the dust of the earth in a measure and weighed
> the mountains in scales and the hills in a balance? Who has
> measured the Spirit of the LORD, or what man shows him his
> counsel? Whom did he consult, and who made him understand?
> Who taught him the path of justice, and taught him knowledge,
> and showed him the way of understanding? Behold, the nations
> are like a drop from a bucket, and are accounted as the dust
> on the scales; behold, he takes up the coastlands like fine dust.
> Lebanon would not suffice for fuel, nor are its beasts enough for a
> burnt offering. All the nations are as nothing before him, they are

accounted by him as less than nothing and emptiness. To whom then will you liken God, or what likeness compare with him? An idol! A craftsman casts it, and a goldsmith overlays it with gold and casts for it silver chains. He who is too impoverished for an offering chooses wood that will not rot; he seeks out a skillful craftsman to set up an idol that will not move. Do you not know? Do you not hear? Has it not been told you from the beginning? Have you not understood from the foundations of the earth? It is he who sits above the circle of the earth, and its inhabitants are like grasshoppers; who stretches out the heavens like a curtain, and spreads them like a tent to dwell in; who brings princes to nothing, and makes the rulers of the earth as emptiness. Scarcely are they planted, scarcely sown, scarcely has their stem taken root in the earth, when he blows on them, and they wither, and the tempest carries them off like stubble. To whom then will you compare me, that I should be like him? says the Holy One. Lift up your eyes on high and see: who created these? He who brings out their host by number, calling them all by name; by the greatness of his might and because he is strong in power, not one is missing. Why do you say, O Jacob, and speak, O Israel, "My way is hidden from the LORD, and my right is disregarded by my God"? Have you not known? Have you not heard? The LORD is the everlasting God, the Creator of the ends of the earth. He does not faint or grow weary; his understanding is unsearchable. He gives power to the faint, and to him who has no might he increases strength. Even youths shall faint and be weary, and young men shall fall exhausted; but they who wait for the Lord shall renew their strength; they shall mount up with wings like eagles; they shall run and not be weary; they shall walk and not faint. (Isaiah 40:10–31)

○ Because of who he is.

> The earth is the LORD's and the fullness thereof, the world and those who dwell therein . . . (Psalm 24:1)

○ Because of what he can do.

Now the whole earth had one language and the same words. And as people migrated from the east, they found a plain in the land of Shinar and settled there. And they said to one another, "Come, let us make bricks, and burn them thoroughly." And they had brick for stone, and bitumen for mortar. Then they said, "Come, let us build ourselves a city and a tower with its top in the heavens, and let us make a name for ourselves, lest we be dispersed over the face of the whole earth." And the LORD came down to see the city and the tower, which the children of man had built. And the LORD said, "Behold, they are one people, and they have all one language, and this is only the beginning of what they will do. And nothing that they propose to do will now be impossible for them. Come, let us go down and there confuse their language, so that they may not understand one another's speech." So the LORD dispersed them from there over the face of all the earth, and they left off building the city. Therefore its name was called Babel, because there the LORD confused the language of all the earth. And from there the LORD dispersed them over the face of all the earth. (Genesis 11:1–9)

The LORD brings the counsel of the nations to nothing; he frustrates the plans of the peoples. (Psalm 33:10)

- God can be trusted to carry out _____ of his good purposes.

I know that you can do all things, and that no purpose of yours can be thwarted. (Job 42:2)

Remember this and stand firm, recall it to mind, you transgressors, remember the former things of old; for I am God, and there is no other; I am God, and there is none like me, declaring the end from the beginning and from ancient times things not yet done, saying, "My counsel shall stand, and I will accomplish all my purpose," calling a bird of prey from the east, the man of my counsel from a far country. I have spoken, and I will bring it to pass; I have purposed, and I will do it. (Isaiah 46:8–11)

And we know that for those who love God all things work together for good, for those who are called according to his purpose. For those whom he foreknew he also predestined to be conformed to the image of his Son, in order that he might be the firstborn among many brothers. And those whom he predestined he also called, and those whom he called he also justified, and those whom he justified he also glorified. (Romans 8:28–30)

Humanity will never be destroyed; humanity will ultimately be _____.

• New birth . . .

> *. . . since you have been born again, not of perishable seed but of imperishable, through the living and abiding word of God . . . (1 Peter 1:23)*

• New identity . . .

> *Therefore, if anyone is in Christ, he is a new creation. The old has passed away; behold, the new has come. (2 Corinthians 5:17)*

> *I have been crucified with Christ. It is no longer I who live, but Christ who lives in me. And the life I now live in the flesh I live by faith in the Son of God, who loved me and gave himself for me. (Galatians 2:20)*

> *To them God chose to make known how great among the Gentiles are the riches of the glory of this mystery, which is Christ in you, the hope of glory. (Colossians 1:27)*

• A new image . . .

> *And we all, with unveiled face, beholding the glory of the Lord, are being transformed into the same image from one degree of glory to another. For this comes from the Lord who is the Spirit. (2 Corinthians 3:18)*

- A new _____ . . .

> But our citizenship is in heaven, and from it we await a Savior, the Lord Jesus Christ, who will transform our lowly body to be like his glorious body, by the power that enables him even to subject all things to himself. (Philippians 3:20–21)

- Followers of Jesus will be completely _____.

> For I consider that the sufferings of this present time are not worth comparing with the glory that is to be revealed to us. (Romans 8:18)

> And not only the creation, but we ourselves, who have the firstfruits of the Spirit, groan inwardly as we wait eagerly for adoption as sons, the redemption of our bodies. For in this hope we were saved. Now hope that is seen is not hope. For who hopes for what he sees? But if we hope for what we do not see, we wait for it with patience. (Romans 8:23–25)

- We will be free from the presence of sin.

> . . . who will sustain you to the end, guiltless in the day of our Lord Jesus Christ. (1 Corinthians 1:8)

> "Let us rejoice and exult and give him the glory, for the marriage of the Lamb has come, and his Bride has made herself ready; it was granted her to clothe herself with fine linen, bright and pure"—for the fine linen is the righteous deeds of the saints. (Revelation 19:7–8)

- We will be conformed into the likeness of Jesus.

> Beloved, we are God's children now, and what we will be has not yet appeared; but we know that when he appears we shall be like him, because we shall see him as he is. (1 John 3:2)

- We will be welcomed into an everlasting kingdom.

> *For in this way there will be richly provided for you an entrance into the eternal kingdom of our Lord and Savior Jesus Christ.* (2 Peter 1:11)

> *The Lord will rescue me from every evil deed and bring me safely into his heavenly kingdom. To him be the glory forever and ever. Amen.* (2 Timothy 4:18)

○ Most Christians will _____.

> *Behold! I tell you a mystery. We shall not all sleep, but we shall all be changed, in a moment, in the twinkling of an eye, at the last trumpet. For the trumpet will sound, and the dead will be raised imperishable, and we shall be changed.* (1 Corinthians 15:51–52)

- For those Christians who die . . .
  - Their bodies are buried in earth.
  - Their souls are welcomed in heaven.

> *So we are always of good courage. We know that while we are at home in the body we are away from the Lord, for we walk by faith, not by sight. Yes, we are of good courage, and we would rather be away from the body and at home with the Lord. So whether we are at home or away, we make it our aim to please him. For we must all appear before the judgment seat of Christ, so that each one may receive what is due for what he has done in the body, whether good or evil.* (2 Corinthians 5:6–10)

> *And he said to him, "Truly, I say to you, today you will be with me in paradise."* (Luke 23:43)

> *And as they were stoning Stephen, he called out, "Lord Jesus, receive my spirit."* (Acts 7:59)

- Death is not the end.

- Death is just the beginning.

○ All Christians will be resurrected.

> *So is it with the resurrection of the dead. What is sown is perishable; what is raised is imperishable. It is sown in dishonor; it is raised in glory. It is sown in weakness; it is raised in power. It is sown a natural body; it is raised a spiritual body. If there is a natural body, there is also a spiritual body. Thus it is written, "The first man Adam became a living being"; the last Adam became a life-giving spirit. But it is not the spiritual that is first but the natural, and then the spiritual. The first man was from the earth, a man of dust; the second man is from heaven. (1 Corinthians 15:42–47)*

- Our bodies will be eternal.
- Our bodies will be beautiful.

> *Then the righteous will shine like the sun in the kingdom of their Father. He who has ears, let him hear. (Matthew 13:43)*

- Our bodies will be powerful.
- Our bodies will be spiritual (permanently Spirit-filled).
- Our bodies will be recognizable.

> *If the Spirit of him who raised Jesus from the dead dwells in you, he who raised Christ Jesus from the dead will also give life to your mortal bodies through his Spirit who dwells in you. (Romans 8:11)*

> *I tell you, many will come from east and west and recline at table with Abraham, Isaac, and Jacob in the kingdom of heaven . . . (Matthew 8:11)*

○ Creation will be completely _____.

> *For the creation waits with eager longing for the revealing of the sons of God. For the creation was subjected to futility, not*

willingly, but because of him who subjected it, in hope that the creation itself will be set free from its bondage to corruption and obtain the freedom of the glory of the children of God. For we know that the whole creation has been groaning together in the pains of childbirth until now. (Romans 8:19–22)

Then I saw a new heaven and a new earth, for the first heaven and the first earth had passed away, and the sea was no more. (Revelation 21:1)

- Heaven: a place of unhindered fellowship with God.

Then I saw a new heaven and a new earth, for the first heaven and the first earth had passed away, and the sea was no more. And I saw the holy city, new Jerusalem, coming down out of heaven from God, prepared as a bride adorned for her husband. And I heard a loud voice from the throne saying, "Behold, the dwelling place of God is with man. He will dwell with them, and they will be his people, and God himself will be with them as their God. He will wipe away every tear from their eyes, and death shall be no more, neither shall there be mourning, nor crying, nor pain anymore, for the former things have passed away." (Revelation 21:1–4)

- We will be with him!
  - Death will be replaced by life.
    - No more sin.
    - No more sorrow.
    - No more sickness.
    - No more separation.

  - Night will be replaced by light.

And I saw no temple in the city, for its temple is the Lord God the Almighty and the Lamb. And the city has no need of sun or moon to shine on it, for the glory of God gives it light, and its lamp is the Lamb. By its light will the nations walk, and the kings of the earth will bring their glory into it, and

> *its gates will never be shut by day—and there will be no night there.* (Revelation 21:22–25)

> *And he who was seated on the throne said, "Behold, I am making all things new." Also he said, "Write this down, for these words are trustworthy and true."* (Revelation 22:5)

- ○ Corruption will be replaced by purity.

> *But nothing unclean will ever enter it, nor anyone who does what is detestable or false, but only those who are written in the Lamb's book of life.* (Revelation 21:27)

- ○ Curse will be replaced by blessing.

> *Then the angel showed me the river of the water of life, bright as crystal, flowing from the throne of God and of the Lamb through the middle of the street of the city; also, on either side of the river, the tree of life with its twelve kinds of fruit, yielding its fruit each month. The leaves of the tree were for the healing of the nations. No longer will there be anything accursed, but the throne of God and of the Lamb will be in it, and his servants will worship him.* (Revelation 22:1–3)

- We will see his _____!

> *They will see his face, and his name will be on their foreheads.* (Revelation 22:4)

- Heaven: a place of indescribable worship of God.

> *Then I heard what seemed to be the voice of a great multitude, like the roar of many waters and like the sound of mighty peals of thunder, crying out, "Hallelujah! For the Lord our God the Almighty reigns. Let us rejoice and exult and*

give him the glory, for the marriage of the Lamb has come, and his Bride has made herself ready; it was granted her to clothe herself with fine linen, bright and pure"—for the fine linen is the righteous deeds of the saints. And the angel said to me, "Write this: Blessed are those who are invited to the marriage supper of the Lamb." And he said to me, "These are the true words of God." (Revelation 19:6–9)

Final Exhortations

Since all these things are thus to be dissolved, what sort of people ought you to be in lives of holiness and godliness, waiting for and hastening the coming of the day of God, because of which the heavens will be set on fire and dissolved, and the heavenly bodies will melt as they burn! But according to his promise we are waiting for new heavens and a new earth in which righteousness dwells. (2 Peter 3:11–13)

- Let's become more like Jesus every _____.

    And we all, with unveiled face, beholding the glory of the Lord, are being transformed into the same image from one degree of glory to another. For this comes from the Lord who is the Spirit. (2 Corinthians 3:18)

- Let's proclaim the gospel of Jesus to every _____.

    And Jesus came and said to them, "All authority in heaven and on earth has been given to me. Go therefore and make disciples of all nations, baptizing them in the name of the Father and of the Son and of the Holy Spirit, teaching them to observe all that I have commanded you. And behold, I am with you always, to the end of the age." (Matthew 28:18–20)

- Let's be ready for Jesus to come back at _____ moment.

I have fought the good fight, I have finished the race, I have kept the faith. Henceforth there is laid up for me the crown of righteousness, which the Lord, the righteous judge, will award to me on that day, and not only to me but also to all who have loved his appearing. (2 Timothy 4:7–8)

. . . so Christ, having been offered once to bear the sins of many, will appear a second time, not to deal with sin but to save those who are eagerly waiting for him. (Hebrews 9:28)

For the Lord himself will descend from heaven with a cry of command, with the voice of an archangel, and with the sound of the trumpet of God. And the dead in Christ will rise first. Then we who are alive, who are left, will be caught up together with them in the clouds to meet the Lord in the air, and so we will always be with the Lord. Therefore encourage one another with these words. (1 Thessalonians 4:16–18)

He who testifies to these things says, "Surely I am coming soon." Amen. Come, Lord Jesus! The grace of the Lord Jesus be with all. Amen. (Revelation 22:20–21)

END NOTES

1. Paul David Tripp, *Do You Believe?: 12 Historic Doctrines to Change Your Everyday Life*. (Wheaton: Crossway, 2021), 231–232.

2. This quote from Juan Sanchez comes from the transcript of an interview with Nancie Guthrie. "Juan Sanchez on Image, Identity, and Idolatry," *Help Me Teach the Bible*, *The Gospel Coalition*, January 10, 2019, www.thegospelcoalition.org/podcasts/help-me-teach-the-bible/juan-sanchez-image-identity-idolatry.

3. This quotation from the American Psychological Association (APA) is taken from an informational guide titled "Key Terms and Concepts in Understanding Gender Diversity and Sexual Orientation Among Students," pp. 20–22. The guide defines the various terms mentioned and can be accessed at https://www.apa.org/pi/lgbt/programs/safe-supportive/lgbt/key-terms.pdf.

4. Martin Luther King, Jr. "Letter from a Birmingham Jail," 1963, accessed January 6, 2022, www.csuchico.edu/iege/_assets/documents/susi-letter-from-birmingham-jail.pdf.

5. "Humans of the Metaverse," accessed January 4, 2022, www.nft-stats.com/collection/humans-of-the-metaverse-1.

6. Katie Canales, "Silicon Valley's Metaverse Will Suck Reality into the Virtual World— and Ostracize Those Who Aren't Plugged In," *Business Insider,* December 4, 2021, www.businessinsider.com/metaverse-zuckerberg-facebook-virtual-world-leave-people-behind-2021-12.

7. Rory Cellan-Jones, "Stephen Hawking Warns Artificial Intelligence Could End Mankind," BBC, December 2, 2014, www.bbc.com/news/technology-30290540.

8. Rosae Martín Peña, "Enhanced Humans: the Avatars of the Future," *OpenMind BBVA*, accessed January 11, 2017, www.bbvaopenmind.com/en/science/bioscience/enhanced-humans-the-avatars-of-the-future/.

9. Walter Isaacson, *The Code Breaker: Jennifer Doudna, Gene Editing, and the Future of the Human Race* (New York: Simon & Schuster, 2021), 325–326.

10. Ibid., xvi.

11. Ibid.

12. Henri R. Manasse, Jr., "The Other Side of the Human Genome," *American Journal of Health-System Pharmacy*, 2005; 62 (10): 1080–1086, www.medscape.com/viewarticle/505755_5.

13. Elaine Biggerstaff and Bonney Lake, "Sanger Was a Eugenicist, and That Can't Be Tolerated," *The Courier-Herald*, May 1, 2019, www.courierherald.com/letters/sanger-was-a-eugenicist-and-that-cant-be-tolerated/.

14. Some parts of this section titled "Who Am I?" draw on the work of Wayne Grudem, *Systematic Theology: An Introduction to Biblical Doctrine*, (Grand Rapids: Zondervan, 1994), 439–450.

15. Augustine, *Confessions*, 1.1.1.

16. Christopher Yuan, "He Made Them Male and Female," *Desiring God*, December 14, 2019, www.desiringgod.org/articles/he-made-them-male-and-female.

17. Ibid.

18. This definition of sin is borrowed from Wayne Grudem, *Systematic Theology*, 490.

19. Henri Blocher, *In the Beginning: The Opening Chapters of Genesis* (Leicester, UK: InterVarsity, 1984), 94; as cited in Richard Phillips, "Man as the Image of God," *The Gospel Coalition*, www.thegospelcoalition.org/essay/man-as-the-image-of-god/.

20. Greg Morse, "You are Totally (Not) Depraved: How to Recover Positive Self-Image," *Desiring God*, May 14, 2018, www.desiringgod.org/articles/you-are-totally-not-depraved.

21. Dr. & Mrs. Howard Taylor, *Hudson Taylor's Spiritual Secret* (Chicago: Moody Press, 1989), 179, 162–163.

22. John Calvin, *Institutes of the Christian Religion,* 3.1.1.

23. Julius Kim, "Inaugurations and Image Bearing," *The Gospel Coalition*, January 20, 2021, www.thegospelcoalition.org/article/inaugurations-image-bearing/.

24. H.B. Charles, "The Message of the Cross," a message delivered at *Together for the Gospel,* 2018.

25. John Murray, *Redemption Accomplished and Applied*, (Grand Rapids: Eerdmans, 1955), 145. As cited in Wayne Grudem, *Systematic Theology*, 753.

26. Aubrey Sequeira, "Re-Thinking Homogeneity: The Biblical Case for Multi-Ethnic Churches," *9Marks*, September 25, 2015, www.9marks.org/article/re-thinking-homogeneity-the-biblical-case-for-multi-ethnic-churches/.

27. Dan Graves, "Francis Grimke's Christian Critique of Slavery," *Christianity.com*, May 3, 2010, www.christianity.com/church/church-history/timeline/1801-1900/francis-grimkes-christian-critique-of-slavery-11630591.html.

28. For statistics on abortion in the U.S. and worldwide, see abort73.com.

29. For these points concerning abortion, see chapter 1 of Greg Koukl, *Precious Unborn Human Persons* (Signal Hill: Stand to Reason Press, 1999).

30. Ibid., 26–27.

31. Randy Alcorn, *Pro-Life Answers to Pro-Choice Arguments* (Colorado Springs: Multnomah Books, 2000), 293.

32. For the wording of the definitions and explanations related to IVF and surrogacy, a number of sources were used. See, for example, Joe Carter, "9 Things You Should Know about Surrogacy," *The Gospel Coalition*, June 6, 2014, www.thegospelcoalition.

org/article/9-things-you-should-know-about-surrogacy; Matthew Lee Anderson and Andrew T. Walker, "Breaking Evangelicalism's Silence on IVF," *The Gospel Coalition*, April 25, 2019, www.thegospelcoalition.org/article/evangelicalisms-silence-ivf; Wayne Grudem, "How IVF Can Be Morally Right," *The Gospel Coalition*, April 25, 2019, www.thegospelcoalition.org/article/ivf-morally-right; Joe Carter, "Basic Bioethics: What Christians Should Know about Surrogacy", *ERLC*, November 16, 2017, https://erlc.com/resource-library/articles/basic-bioethics-what-christians-should-know-about-surrogacy/; Albert Mohler, "Christian Morality and Test Tube Babies, Part 1," September 9, 2004, albertmohler.com/2004/09/09/christian-morality-and-test-tube-babies-part-one-3.

33. Helmut Thielicke, "The Borderline Situation of Extreme Conflict," in *Readings in Christian Ethics, Volume 1: Theory and Method* (Grand Rapids: Baker Books, 1994), 127–128.

34. Some of the points regarding encouragement amidst fertility are adapted from Courtney Reissig, "Don't Waste Your Infertility," *The Gospel Coalition*, January 23, 2012, https://www.thegospelcoalition.org/article/dont-waste-your-infertility.

35. Regarding the experience of infertility, these points are taken from the following article: Kimberly Monroe and Philip Monroe, "The Bible and the Pain of Infertility," *Journal of Biblical Counseling* 23:1 (Spring 2005), 50–58. The Christian Counseling and Educational Foundation (CCEF) gave permission to make the article available at abbafund.files.wordpress.com/2010/01/the-bible-and-the-pain-of-infertility1.pdf.

36. For the wording of the definitions and explanations related to genomics and eugenics, a number of sources were used. See, for example, Joe Carter, "The FAQs: What Christians Should Know about CRISPR Genetic Scissors," *The Gospel Coalition*, October 14, 2020, /www.thegospelcoalition.org/article/the-faqs-what-christians-should-know-about-crispr-genetic-scissors; Joe Carter, "The FAQs: Chinese Scientist Claims First Gene-Edited Babies," *The Gospel Coalition*, December 1, 2018, www.thegospelcoalition.org/article/the-faqs-chinese-scientist-claims-first-gene-edited-babies; Joe Carter, "9 Things You Should Know about Eugenics," *The Gospel Coalition*, July 25, 2017, www.thegospelcoalition.org/article/9-things-you-should-know-about-eugenics.

37. Joe Carter, "The FAQs: What Christians Should Know about CRISPR Genetic Scissors," *The Gospel Coalition*, October 14, 2020, /www.thegospelcoalition.org/article/the-faqs-what-christians-should-know-about-crispr-genetic-scissors.

38. Ibid.

39. Ibid.

40. For definitions related to eugenics, see Joe Carter, "9 Things You Should Know about Eugenics," *The Gospel Coalition*, July 25, 2017, www.thegospelcoalition.org/article/9-things-you-should-know-about-eugenics.

41. Ibid.

42. Isaacson, *The Code Breaker*, 294.

43. Ibid., 326–327.

44. Ibid., 335–336.

45. Ibid., 363.

46. Ibid., 348–349.

47. Ibid., 351.

48. Ibid., 364.

49. Ibid., 277.

50. Ibid., 353.

51. Ibid., 354.

52. Ibid., 480–481.

53. For the wording of the definitions and explanations related to Artificial Intelligence (AI) and transhumanism, a number of sources were used. See, for example, the many helpful articles on AI at jasonthacker.com, including Jason Thacker, "What is Artificial Intelligence?" February 20, 2018, jasonthacker.com/2018/02/20/what-is-artificial-intelligence/. See also Jacob Shatzer, "New Year, New You? The Allure of Transhumanism," *The Gospel Coalition*, January 8, 2019, www.thegospelcoalition.org/article/allure-transhumanism.

54. Cited in Samuel D. James, "Into the Metaverse," *First Things*, November 16, 2021, www.firstthings.com/web-exclusives/2021/11/into-the-metaverse.

55. This definition is adapted from Thacker, "What is Artificial Intelligence?" February 20, 2018, jasonthacker.com/2018/02/20/what-is-artificial-intelligence/.

56. Peña, "Enhanced Humans," *OpenMind BBVA*, January 11, 2017, www.bbvaopenmind.com/en/science/bioscience/enhanced-humans-the-avatars-of-the-future/.

57. Cellan-Jones, "Stephen Hawking Warns Artificial Intelligence Could End Mankind," www.bbc.com/news/technology-30290540.

58. This statement from the Ethics & Religious Liberty Commission (ERLC) of the Southern Baptist Convention is titled "Artificial Intelligence: An Evangelical Statement of Principles," and can be accessed at erlc.com/resource-library/statements/artificial-intelligence-an-evangelical-statement-of-principles/.

59. For the wording of the definitions and explanations related to the Metaverse (AI) and digital and social media, a number of sources were used. See, for example, the following: Samuel James, "Into the Metaverse," *First Things*, November 16, 2021, www.firstthings.com/web-exclusives/2021/11/into-the-metaverse; Ian Harber and Patrick Miller, "How to Prepare for the Metaverse," *The Gospel Coalition*, November 2, 2021, www.thegospelcoalition.org/article/prepare-metaverse.

60. This definition is taken from dictionary.com

61. This definition is taken from merriam-webster.com.

62. This definition from Matthew Ball is cited in Ian Harber and Patrick Miller, "How to Prepare for the Metaverse," *The Gospel Coalition*, November 2, 2021, www.thegospelcoalition.org/article/prepare-metaverse.

63. Harber and Miller, "How to Prepare for the Metaverse," www.thegospelcoalition.org/article/prepare-metaverse.

64. Cited in James, "Into the Metaverse," www.firstthings.com/web-exclusives/2021/11/into-the-metaverse.

65. This definition is taken from merriam-webster.com.

66. This definition is taken from merriam-webster.com.

67. A.W. Tozer, *The Knowledge of the Holy: The Attributes of God: Their Meaning in the Christian Life* (San Francisco: HarperCollins, 1961), 1.

68. Ibid., 4.

ABOUT DAVID PLATT

David Platt serves as Lead Pastor of McLean Bible Church in Washington, D.C. He is the founder and chairman of Radical, a ministry that exists to equip the church to be on mission. Resources from David Platt and Radical can be found at radical.net.

David Platt is the author of *Radical*, *Radical Together*, *Follow Me*, *Counter Culture*, *Something Needs to Change*, and *Before You Vote*, and he is the author of several volumes in the Christ-Centered Exposition Commentary series.

David Platt received his Ph.D. from New Orleans Baptist Theological Seminary. Along with his wife and children, he lives in the Washington, D.C. metro area.

ABOUT RADICAL

Jesus calls us to make his glory known among all nations by making disciples and multiplying churches. Being on mission is not simply a compartmentalized program in the church, but the calling of our lives as Christians.

However, 3.2 billion people are currently unreached with the gospel, and many of them endure unimaginable suffering. And, only 1% of missions dollars and 3% of missionaries go to the unreached. Something has to change.

Radical exists to equip the church to be on mission.

We do this by providing:
- Biblical resources to help develop mature Christians and healthy churches
- Trusted avenues to financially support work among the unreached
- Sound training to go effectively to the unreached

To learn more or get involved, go to radical.net.

NOTES